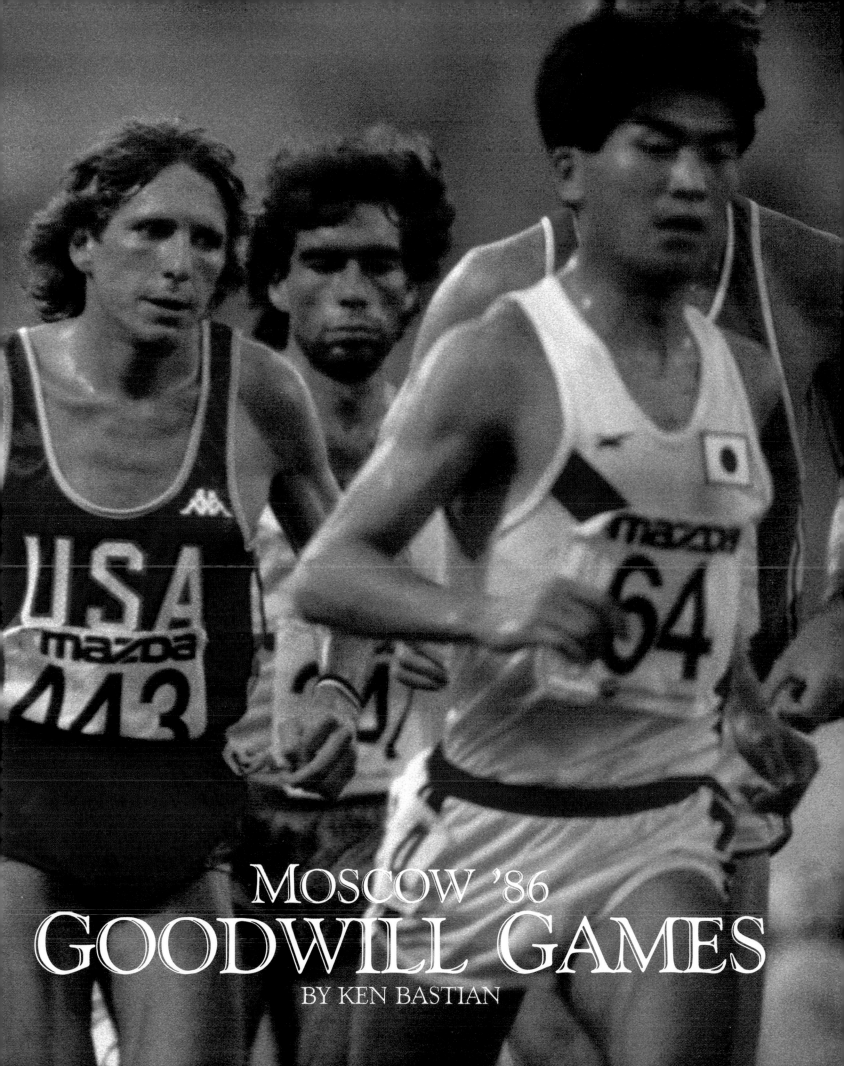

Moscow '86
Goodwill Games

BY KEN BASTIAN

PREFACE

The inaugural Goodwill Games were, in both name and deed, a purveyor of the message that spirited competition among the athletes of the world can enhance goodwill among nations. While peace remains an elusive goal, each person who participated in the Goodwill Games can give testimony to the camaraderie that was fostered on the playing fields of the Soviet Union in July 1986.

Long before the Opening Ceremony, Olympic heroes and world record holders from five continents toured the world together as Goodwill Ambassadors. Speaking through the international language of sport, they broke down barriers, destroyed myths, shared victories, reviewed defeats and touched hearts. The settings for such renderings ranged from orphanages in Frankfurt and hospitals in Madrid to international schools in Tokyo and inner-city schools in Boston. Thousands of young people visited by the Goodwill Ambassadors saw first-hand that the same athletes who hone their skills to defeat each other also, through intense competition, strengthen their friendships .

The Goodwill Ambassadors also took their message of friendship through sportsmanship to the halls of government. In Washington, D.C., Soviet Victor Saneyev, Olympic triple jump gold medalist during the 1970's, couldn't believe he was in the White House meeting Vice President George Bush. Nor could current triple jump world record holder Willie Banks believe *he* was in the White House meeting his Soviet idol, Victor Saneyev.

In Los Angeles, before meeting with Mayor Tom Bradley, Soviet Olympic champion Lyudmilla Bragina paid a nostalgic visit to the L.A. Coliseum, the 1969 site of her first 1,500 meters triumph in international competition. Reminded that this was also the site of the 1984 Olympics, she mused, "The Olympic Games and the Goodwill Games give us twice the opportunity to better get to know and understand each other." In the meeting which followed, Bragina elaborated, "It's time we start making positive strides toward some kind of understanding between the nations of the world. If the Goodwill Games are not the solution, they are at least a beginning."

The following pages bear witness to that beginning. They are a tribute to the remarkable athletes who spoke to us before and after the Opening Ceremony in a language of strength and grace which is shared by us all.

Ken Bastian

This book is dedicated with love and respect to my father, Kenneth H. Bastian, Sr., who was one of the greatest natural athletes I had the privilege of competing against, and one of the truest sportsmen I had the honor of knowing. And to my mother, Ann Winslow Bastian, who continues to teach by example that victory with poise and humility is equal to defeat with dignity and optimism.

CREDITS

This book is a joint venture between The Publishing Group, Atlanta, Georgia (Bevilaqua International, Inc.; Jennings and Associates, Inc.; Marmac Publishing Company, Inc.) and Turner Broadcasting System, Inc., Atlanta, Georgia.

Publishers: John Bevilaqua, Larry Jennings, and Marge McDonald

Executive Editor: Marge McDonald

Written by: Ken Bastian

Photo Captions: Ken Bastian
Susie Blackmun
Kim Bohuny

Photographers: American:
William Hart
Dan Helms/Duomo Photography
Phil Huber/Sports Illustrated
Adam Loory/Sailing World
Kelly Mills
Barbara Y.E. Pyle
Corky Trewin

Soviet:
Robert I. Mairnov/Fizkultura Sport Publishing
David Makchmob/Fizkultura Sport Publishing
Yuri Sokolov/Fizkultura Sport Publishing

Photographers' Assistants: Dan Bliss
Alec Guroff

Editors: Susie Blackmun
Steven Haworth

Associate Editor: Russell Supplee

Photo Editors: Ken Bastian
John Bevilaqua
Susie Blackmun
William Brown
Sharron Safriet
Rosemary Wussler

Contributing Editors: Harriet Glascow
Ann Woods

Production Editor: Kathleen Shaw

Design Direction: Sharron Safriet
Safriet & Chance/Atlanta, Georgia

Designers: Safriet & Chance/Atlanta, Georgia
Clare Ahern
Paula Chance

Typography: Barbara Curtis

Color Separations: G & L Graphics/ Atlanta, Georgia

Printing: Hunter Publishing Co., Winston-Salem, N.C.

Special Thanks: A. Brown-Olmstead & Associates
Arnold Drapkin/Time Magazine
Fuji, USA
U.S. Amateur Sports Federations and Associations

We would like to pay a tribute to all of the members of the TBS team whose collective and tireless efforts made the Goodwill Games' dream into a memorable reality. A sincere note of appreciation also to TBS Vice President for Sports, Rex Lardner; Executive Producer, Don Ellis; Coordinating Producer, Ken Fouts; Managing Editor, David Raith; Vice President for Communications, Arthur Sando; Director of Public Relations, Mike Oglesby; and Creative Director, Vivian LaWand; their invaluable leadership, friendship and assistance which led directly to this publication were an inspiration to everyone involved. A final and special word of graditude for the editorial contributions made by TBS sportscasters, Bob Neal and Craig Sager; expert commentators, Peggy Fleming and Jennifer Chandler; and Director of Research, Kim Bohuny.

Copyright 1986 by Turner Broadcasting System Inc.
First Printing 1986. All rights reserved.
Library of Congress number: 86-062883
ISBN number: 0-939944-47-2
ISSN number: 0736-8200
Distributed in the USA by Pelican Publishing Company, 1101 Monroe Street, Gretna, La. 70053. Distributed internationally by Proost & Brandt Distribution BV, 63 Strijkviertel, 3454 PK De Meern, The Netherlands. Copies of this book may be purchased directly from Marmac Publishing Company, 3423 Piedmont Road, Suite 212, Atlanta, Ga. 30305. 404-231-1153

CONTENTS

See final page for opening photograph identification.

470 champions Morgan Reeser and Kevin Burnham
execute a perfect roll gybe at the leeward mark.

FOREWORD

by Ted Turner

The 1986 Goodwill Games with the Soviets found us with a challenge to demonstrate to the world that we could work toward a mutual goal.

Through our shared language and love of sport, we found a means to communicate our goal for peace and understanding. Through our relationship and throughout our telecast we endeavored to show the world that what our nations have in common far surpasses our differences.

For those of you who were with us during our coverage of the Games, we tried to take you beyond the competitors' lives on the field to acquaint you with their customs, and daily routines at home, with their friends and families. We wanted to offer you the opportunity to get to know, and better understand, other people as people.

The journey to mutual understanding begins with but a single step. It is the hope of Turner Broadcasting System and our Soviet colleagues that the inaugural Goodwill Games have provided our world a purposeful step forward on that journey.

Ted Turner, President and Chairman of the Board, Turner Broadcasting System, Inc.

American gymnast and Goodwill
Ambassador, Tim Daggett.

INTRODUCTION

by Robert J. Wussler

On a hot July afternoon in 1984, I found a rare moment in the midst of a hectic day to catch a glimpse of the Olympics on television. That moment was promptly interrupted by Ted Turner. Charging into my office he frantically pointed at my television monitor. "We've got to do something about this, Wussler," he said, referring to the Soviets' absence in Los Angeles. "We've got to get the Americans and the Soviets...No, we've got to get *everyone* competing together again, and get the politics out of sport." Forty-eight hours later, I was on my way to Moscow as the emissary of Ted Turner's dream of uniting the world once again on the field of play.

One year and countless hours of negotiation later, on August 6, 1985, I signed a joint agreement with Henrikus Yushkiavitshus, Vice-Chairman of the Soviet State Committee on Television and Radio, and Vjacheslav Gavrilin, Vice-Chairman of the Soviet Committee on Physical Culture and Sport, to organize, stage and televise the 1986 Goodwill Games. Ted Turner's dream was becoming a reality, but we were left with less than a year to accomplish what Olympic organizers do in the space of five years.

In ten short months, we orchestrated one of the most complicated athletic events and broadcasts in television history. Television engineers, programming people and producers from different countries and all walks of life worked together to build a state-of-the-art broadcast center in Moscow. We added another broadcast venue in Madrid for coverage of the Men's World Basketball Championship. American and international sports federations played a critical role in attracting more than 3,000 athletes from a world of scattered athletic interests. Sixty-seven independent television stations across America, and foreign television networks around the world, brought the Games into the homes of people on five continents.

There was one primary source of motivation that helped us all meet our challenge – the lofty purpose of the Games. Perhaps is was best summarized by Mr. Yushkiavitshus during the signing of our agreement: "It is far better for us to meet on the playing fields than it is for us to meet on the battlefields.

Robert J. Wussler – Executive Vice President, Turner Broadcasting System, Inc.; President, SuperStation WTBS; and General Manager, 1986 Goodwill Games.

OPENING CEREMONY

High-flying aerialists, "hovering spaceships" and glittering fireworks ushered in a renewed era of good-will among athletes and nations.

An opening ceremonies crowd 103,000 strong was thoroughly entertained for three specta-cular hours by an ever-changing, brightly-colored sea of festive dancers, juggling clowns and tumbling gymnasts. The 21,000 performers on the field of Lenin Stadium ranged in style and diversity from the Bolshoi Ballet to the Moscow Circus – all beneath an 11,000-member card section flashing a moving mosaic of 51 separate images depicting symbols of global peace and harmony.

The orchestral mastery of Soviet producers Valentin Voronov and Leonid Monastyrsky reached its zenith as 2,800 dancers and gymnasts joined at mid-field in a 30-foot human visage of a glimmering torch. Rising in magnificence through the card section, the torch's image surged to the very top of Lenin Stadium to coincide perfectly with the actual lighting of the Goodwill Flame. Symbolizing peace and brother-hood, the flame would burn for 16 glorious days and nights to celebrate a long-awaited reunion of the world's athletic elite.

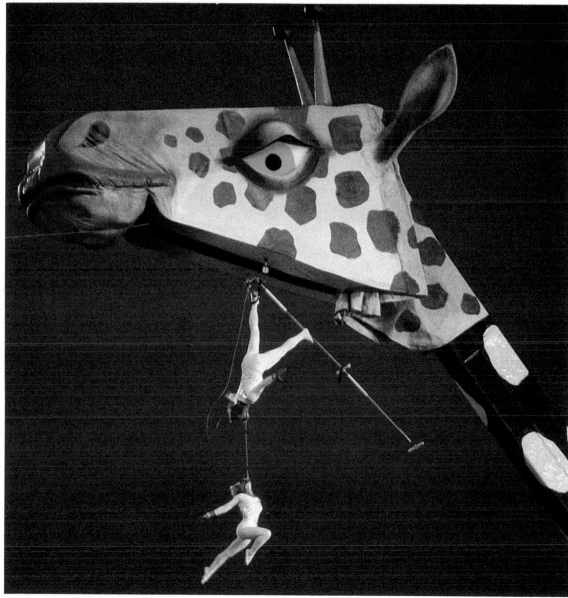

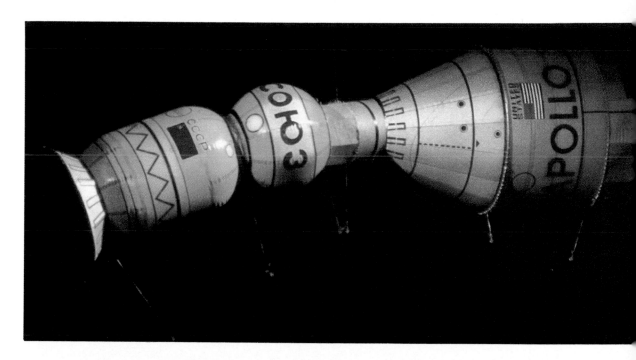

THE
COMPETITION

Jackie Joyner's personal best in the long jump helped make her the world's best in the heptathlon.

THE COMPETITION

"I've had a good feeling since the Opening Ceremony," said U.S. heptathlete Jackie Joyner. "People have been very warm. And tonight you heard a predominately Soviet crowd pulling for an American to set the world record. That tells me something."

As Jackie Joyner stretched her weary legs just before her final event in the heptathlon – the 800 meters – the P.A. announcer boomed, in an unmistakably Russian accent, "We all hope Jackie Joyner will make it."

Joyner dug in her spikes for the start. She needed a time of 2:24.64. In the stands, her husband and coach Bob Kersee buried his head in his hands, unable to watch. Two minutes and 10.02 seconds later, Kersee peeked through his fingers to see his wife burst across the finish line to become the world's best all-around female athlete. The crowd roared its approval as the new world record holder, waving a red rose high in the air, made her victory lap while Kersee celebrated his wife's triumph with a victory dance of his own. "To do what Jackie has done is almost unheard of," he raved. "This is one of those magical moments in an athlete's life."

The reunion of 3,000 members of the world's athletic family was made even more dramatic when the athletes' *own* family members shared in the magic. On opening day of the competition after the USSR's Vladimir Salnikov set a world record in the 800 meters, his jubilant teammates tossed his wife Marina – who is also his coach – into the pool. There, to the delight of her husband and the cheering crowd, a soggy Mrs. Salnikov smothered her star pupil with hugs and kisses of victory. Two days later Soviet polevault star Sergei Bubka, who had promised his son Vitaly a world record in celebration of his first birthday, delivered the gift by improving his own world mark to 19'8¾". The following week, 3-month-old American Alexander Schultz found himself triumphantly held high atop the victory stand by his father, Olympic and World Champion wrestler Dave Schultz, who had just moments before captured another gold medal to add to his impressive collection.

From the opening day of swimming to the closing day of judo, six world records were shattered and 181 gold medals were awarded in competition highlighted by international and immediate family unity. That spirit was exemplified by U.S. swimmer Janet Evans and Soviet 400-meter hurdler Aleksandr Vasilyev. Evans, the youngest and smallest member of the U.S. swimming team, awarded the larger-than-life Salnikov a lacquered tray emblazoned in gold with her team's official seal in tribute to the Soviet's 21 world records. Vasilyev honored American Edwin Moses' 111th straight win with a hand-painted Russian memento which he presented to the American in the U.S. dressing room only minutes after Moses had defeated him.

The hopes and dreams of all these family members – including officials, organizers and athletes representing 79 countries – were best expressed by one of the Games' most seasoned competitors, Olympic Champion and U.S. volleyball team captain Karch Kiraly: "In a major event like the Goodwill Games, people see the significance of the USA and the USSR going at it. But to us, it's one great team against another great team. There is mutual respect, player to player. We pride ourselves on having hard-fought, well-played contests. We also get along better than any other teams in the world." Let the Goodwill Games competition begin!

*Vadim Jaroshhuk of the Soviet Union
won the 200m and 400m individual medleys.*

Swimming

While the Statue of Liberty was being unveiled amidst Independence Day fanfare thousands of miles away back home, any hopes for celebrating by the American swimming team in Moscow seemed even more distant. Only five of the 40 U.S. swimmers had tested the waters of international competition. Experts predicted that it would take a miracle to keep this team from foundering in the wake of the perennial powers from the Soviet Union and the German Democratic Republic.

As the starter's gun sounded, a miracle came in the form of an angel from Americus, Georgia. Nineteen-year-old Angel Myers ignited the U.S. squad by shattering the American record in the 50-meter freestyle and taking home the first-ever gold medal in Goodwill Games history. Minutes after Angel stepped out of the pool, teammate John Sauerland touched-out Soviet Gennadi Prigoda for the gold in the men's 50-meter freestyle. Their victories became contagious as the U.S. women responded with another gold in the 4 x 100 relay and an astounding medal sweep, led by Kathy Hettche's gold, in the 800-meter freestyle.

Yet even the Fourth of July miracles performed by the Americans could not outshine the individual brilliance of Soviet swimming treasure Vladimir Salnikov, who dazzled the opening day crowd with a world record (7:50.64) in the men's 800-meter freestyle. The legendary Salnikov satisfied the experts in dramatic fashion by stroking in under his own world mark by two full seconds.

The final days of swimming drama, however, belonged to America's Sean Killian. Competing in his first international meet, the recent high school graduate stunned the swimming world by dethroning his idol, Salnikov, in the 400-meter freestyle. Killian's heroics and Angel Myers' three additional golds sparked the fireworks for an American team total of 15 gold medals — to the Soviets' 12 — in a competition which ended as miraculously as it had begun.

"The angel from Americus." A stunning performance by Angel Myers brought home four gold medals and one bronze.

Soviet Vladimir Salnikov waves to the crowd after breaking another world record, this time in the 800m freestyle.

Since swimming into international competition in 1977, Salnikov has broken 21 world records.

American Sean Killian raises his arms in victory after defeating his idol, Salnikov, in the 400m freestyle.

Kathy Hettche was one of the "Fourth of July miracles," winning an Independence Day gold for her country.

Romanian Noemi Lung stokes to the gold in the women's 200m individual medley.

Birte Weigang (GDR) flew to victory in the 100m butterfly.

Elena Volkova powers to a 200m breaststroke championship.

The U.S. team took the silver medal in the men's 4 x 100m relay.

Aneta Patarasciou from Romania prepares to take off toward victory in the 200m backstroke.

With individual displays of power and determination the U.S. swimmers stroked to 49 swimming medals.

John Witchell, 200m freestylist, rests after winning an Amercian gold.

Igor Polyansky, called "The Log" by his teammates, captured both the 100m and 200m backstroke.

Setting his sights skyward, Doug Padilla "kicks past" teammate Terry Brahm (USA-386) who strains to outlast Eugeuhi Ignatov (337-BUL) for a sparkling gold-silver U.S. finish in the 5,000m.

ATHLETICS (TRACK & FIELD)

The stars over Lenin Stadium shone brightly upon the Olympic Games in 1980, but missing then were many of the stars on the field who would dazzle the Goodwill Games in 1986. Led by the spectacular Sergei Bubka, the Soviets would win two more gold medals than the U.S.; but for 1980 Olympians Edwin Moses and Doug Padilla, heptathlete Jackie Joyner, and their American teammates, it seemed that a once-in-a-lifetime moment had been recreated so that they too could shine beneath the Russian sky. . . and how they did shine!

The peerless Moses extended his lofty winning streak to 111 as he blazed for the gold in the 400-meter hurdles – his dominance in his event unparalleled in track and field history. World Cup Champion Padilla's meteoric kick in the final stretch of the men's 5,000 meters dusted off countryman Terry Brahm for a sparkling 1-2 U.S. finish. In the 100-meter sprint, world record-holder Evelyn Ashford shot past the GDR's Heike Drechsler at the tape to grab the gold in a photo-finish. High jumper Doug Nordquist soared to a personal best of 7'8" in his first win over Soviet world record-holder Igor Paklin. And track and field's new first lady, Joyner, sparkled day *and* night to amass a seven-event total which surpassed the world record by a stunning 202 points. Not since the incomparable Babe Didrikson had an American woman performed with such magnificence.

Also stunning was Canadian Ben Johnson's defeat of American Carl Lewis in the 100 meters. Johnson's gold medal time (9.95) was the fastest non-altitude time ever run; Lewis had to settle for a bronze behind Nigeria's silver medalist Chidi Imoh. Undaunted, Lewis returned to recapture the lead in the 4 x 100-meter relay to bring home the gold for his team.

The 10,000-meter race was also highlighted by a team effort as the Portuguese Castro brothers, Domingos and Dionisio, raced to a dazzling gold-bronze family finish.

In the pole vault, Sergei Bubka launched himself into track and field immortality as he eclipsed his own world record for the sixth consecutive time. After Bubka landed from his 19' 8¾" ascent, his first ever world record in his homeland, he was asked if he knew that Americans considered him to be the USSR's second most notable personality. Bubka replied, "Who's the first?" It was a fitting answer for the gifted young Soviet, who joined the stars on the field to shine as never before beneath the Russian sky.

After capturing the gold in the 100 meters, a beaming Evelyn Ashford (USA) is congratulated by bronze medalist Elvira Barbashina (USSR).

An ecstatic family finish in the 10,000-meter race saw gold and bronze medals awarded to the Castro brothers of Portugal. Domingos (347) and Dionisio (348) flank American Gerard Donakowski (387), who took the silver.

Robert Emmiyan captured the long jump gold for the USSR.

The ever-present track and field judge

When Sergei Bubka, with a leap of 19' 8¾", broke his own world record for the sixth time, it finally happened in his homeland.

Canadian Ben Johnson (467) upset American Carl Lewis (378) in the 100 meters. Nigeria's Chidi Imoh (481) also sneaked past Lewis for the silver.

Carl Lewis anchored his American teammates Harvey Glance, Lee McRae and Floyd Heard to victory.

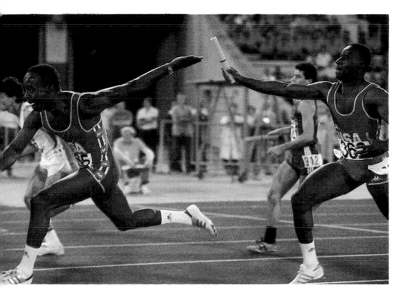

Lee McRae's handoff to Floyd Heard shows the split second precision needed in the relay. (reverse angle)

American Doug Nordquist squeeks over a 7'8" high jump for a personal best and a gold medal.

Greg Foster (USA-389), well on his way to victory in the 110m hurdles, edges out Aleksandr Markin (USSR-216) and Igor Kazanov (USSR-196).

Heading for the tape in the 800 meters,
Johnny Gray (381) blasts by
Kenya's Nixon Kiprotich (454)

American high jumper Doug Nordquist is ecstatic after his first win over Soviet world record holder Igor Paklin.

Soviet Marianna Maslennikova prepares to launch her javelin in the heptathlon competition.

Domingo Menargues of Spain braces himself for a dunking during the steeplechase.

Powerful Bill Green prepares to unleash a throw in the hammer competition.

After a disappointing '84 Olympic finish, Tom Petranoff restored his reputation by winning the javelin gold.

A peerless Edwin Moses
prepares for his 111th
consecutive win in
the 400m hurdles.

Jackie Joyner, with efforts like this, broke the world record formerly held by GDR's Sabine Paetz.

Kristine Tannander of Sweden "reaches back" in the javelin competition.

Jackie Joyner, new first lady of track and field, basks in the glory of her world record.

Natalia Grigoryeva (URS) has only one thought on her mind as she speeds toward the next hurdle.

Elena Davydova (URS) is disappointed by her long jump performance in the women's heptathlon.

America's Diane Dixon sprints for the home-stretch in the 400m.

U.S. women's 4x100m relay team on the winners' stand, flanked by Soviet silver and bronze medalists.

Margareta Keszeg of Romania sets the pace in the women's 1500m.

On your mark!

World record-holder Evelyn Ashford is air-borne as she sprints to the gold medal in the 100m.

Soviet marathon runners Nikolai Ivanov (110) Aleksandr Khlynin (147) and Sergei Krestyaninov (112) keep up the pace.

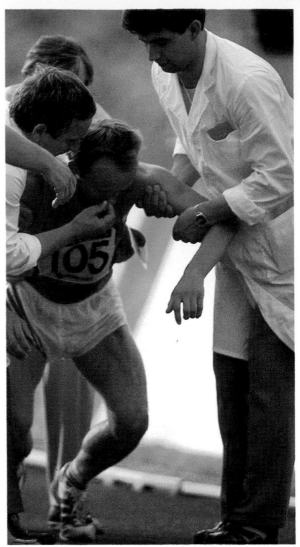

An exhausted Dimitri Feijtistiv (URS) gets a dose of smelling salts after finishing tenth in the marathon.

The top three American marathoners – Julie Isphording (695) Katy Laetsch Schilly (697) and Maureen Custy (685).

G. Belaine Dinsamo brings glory to Ethiopia as he heads for the tape and the gold in the men's marathon.

Sweden's Stefan Blomstrond clears another height in the decathlon's pole vault.

Decathlon silver medalist Aleksandr Apaichev of the USSR.

Garrett Armstrong (256-USA) overtakes Aleksei Lyakh (213-URS) for a 100m first-place finish.

im Bright (262-USA) outdistanced Tomas Faner (426-GDR) and Aleksei Lyakh (213-URS) in the decathlon's 110m hurdles.

A determined Cindy Bremser (681) challenges a tiring Elena Zhupiyeva (USSR-677) in the women's 3,000 meters.

The agony of defeat.

Clarissa Davis and Cheryl Miller skyrocket over the Soviets as they battle for a rebound.

WOMEN'S BASKETBALL

"ON A MISSION FOR THE GOLD"

by the 1986 U.S. Women's Basketball Team

"It started in April at Colorado Springs,
Where a bunch of young ladies started to hustle a team.
The hustle, the sweat was all over the place;
They worked very hard to represent their States.

There were many young ladies that vanished without a trace,
But twelve were left to represent the USA.
The Goodwill Games gathered a lot of attention,
And these twelve ladies are on a mission.

We're on a mission for the gold –
We're going for first, not second, not third.
These twelve young ladies are very unique,
'Cause they rocked the house and never settled for defeat."

That's how the soulful U.S. women hoopsters got themselves sky-high before taking the home court advantage and the Goodwill Games gold from the USSR women in a frenzied 83-60 finale. How sky-high? High enough to break the Soviets' ionospheric 152-game winning streak extending over 28 years of major international competition.

There were high-fives everywhere as Cheryl Miller, Anne Donovan & Co. caught fire midway through the first half to outscore the World Champions 20-4, dancing and prancing to a hand-slapping 14-point lead. The rest of the half was for the record book, as 6'8" Donovan dotted the "i" in history with her "stuff" of a sweeping hook shot by 7' 1¾" Iuliana Semenova. In response, a wildly inspired U.S. cheering section treated their Soviet hosts to the first-ever "spectator wave" in the USSR.

A half-time break concluded, Katrina McClain (17 points, 9 rebounds), Teresa Edwards (13 points, 7 assists) and Miller (18 points, 10 rebounds) brought it all home – by dominating the boards and filling the lanes with playground grit and NBA grace – for the gold!

U.S. point guard Kamie Ethridge (5 assists) put her team's "run and gun" victory into perspective when she concluded, "They played about as poorly as they can, and we played about as well as we can." The Soviet women somehow understood. They received their silver medal with the same grace they have displayed for so many decades as winners of the gold.

The bronze medalists from Brazil also stood with pride and poise on the medal platform. Earlier in the evening, they earned an impressive 87-66 win over Czechoslovakia, behind the tournament's leading scorers Hortencia Marcari and Maria da Silva.

For the gold medalists, however, it was the tournament's third leading scorer, Cheryl Miller, who best symbolized the style and substance of her "hip," yet patriotic, teammates. She had arrived wearing green-tinted shades and a walkman, but departed wrapped in an American flag.

A determined Kamie Ethridge sets up the offense.

Yugoslavia's Jelica Komnenovic shoots over USA's Cindy Brown (6) and Cynthia Cooper (14).

The formidable Cheryl Miller squeezes between two of Brazil's mightiest.

Katrina McClain soars inside for two of her gold medal game 17 points.

Lyudmila Muravyova congratulates U.S. team captain Kamie Ethridge after the Soviets were devastated by the Americans in the championship match.

Soviet giant Iuliana Semenova (10) towers over Anne Donovan (7) and the court.

The reigning Queen of the
court, Cheryl Miller. displays
her golden touch.

From Russia with love.

Teresa Edwards focuses on defense to play her part in "the mission for the gold."

Arvidas Sabonis' slam-dunk ignites a Soviet rally in Madrid.

MEN'S BASKETBALL

The best 24 amateur basketball teams in the world dispersed to four different sites in Spain to begin competition for the 10th World Basketball Championship. When TBS first announced that television coverage of the Championship would be incorporated into the Goodwill Games' broadcast, it was widely assumed that there would be a showdown in Madrid between the United States and the Soviet Union. Instead, the semifinal game against the USSR found Yugoslavia poised to play the role of "giant-killer."

With 55 seconds remaining, Yugoslavia has reached a comfortable nine-point lead over the Soviet World Champions, 85-76. A prior U.S. defeat of Brazil means a USA-Yugoslavia showdown for the 1986 World Championship. . . if the Yugoslavs can hold on.

Fifty seconds left. The USSR's 7'2" star, Arvidas Sabonis, banks home a three-pointer from the top of the key, to make it 85-79.

The Soviets come up with a steal and Valeri Tikhonenko nails another three-pointer from the left side, 85-82.

Thirteen seconds left. The Soviets foul and the Yugoslavs' 18 year-old, seven-foot Vladimir Divac double dribbles off the inbounds pass at mid-court. Soviets' ball, still down by three.

Four seconds left. Inbounds pass to Valdis Valters on the left side. Valters hits another three-pointer. Overtime!

Sabonis (25 points) knocks in two consecutive one-and-ones from the foul line to cap an astonishing Soviet comeback. USSR 91, Yugoslavia 90. It's the Soviets against the Americans for the World Championship.

Eight minutes remaining and the U.S. has built a commanding 18-point lead over the Soviets, 78-60. Sabonis (16 points, 11 rebounds) jams twice to begin a Soviet rally.

USA's guard Tyrone "Mugsey" Bogues (10 steals, 5 assists), forward Charles Smith (17 points) and center David Robinson (20 points) remember a page of basketball history: *1985 World University Games, the USSR's Valdemaras Khomichus hits at the buzzer to beat the U.S. by two.*

Fifty-two seconds to play. The same Khomichus hits his 10th straight point to cut the U.S. lead to two, 85-83.

USA's Kenny Smith (21 points) remembers another history lesson: *1982 World Championship Game, the USA's Doc Rivers misses an open jumpshot at the buzzer – the USSR over the U.S. by one point.*

Forty seconds remaining and Smith makes his move inside, up. . . over Sabonis. . . scores! 87-83.

Sixteen seconds to go. Soviet forward Rimas Kurtinaytis powers for the tip-in. 87-85.

U.S. Coach Lute Olson remembers the 1972 Olympics: *the USSR throws the ball the length of the court for a tip-in at the buzzer. The USSR by one.*

Four seconds left, the U.S. blows the inbounds pass after a foul. Out of timeouts, the USSR throws the ball the length of the court to Aleksandr Volkov in the lane. Volkov turns, Volkov shoots. . . Volkov misses.

The U.S. adds a new page to basketball history: *World Champion USA 87, silver medalist USSR 85.*

Ecstatic U.S. fans followed their team all the way to Oviedo.

Star Soviet player, the 7'2" Arvidas Sabonis, shoots over USA's 6'11" David Robinson.

Kenny Smith's (7) goal helped lead the United States to Madrid for the final four. "Mugsey" Bogues looks on.

David Robinson (11-USA) battles for a rebound over the Brazilians.

Arvidas Sabonis "stuffs" over Yugoslavia in the semi-finals.

The pride of America's team, flyweight
Arthur Johnson, goes after Soviet
Rinvidas Bilus to capture the only
U.S. gold medal.

BOXING

Throughout the boxing competition, the music from the gymnastics floor exercises could often be heard through the partition of the Olympic Sports Complex indoor stadium. The USSR's boxing fans had much to cheer about at the Goodwill Games, but felt little need to be vociferous about it. They calmly watched as Soviet boxers methodically filled 20 of the 24 berths in the finals.

Only American flyweight champion Arthur Johnson was able to break the Soviet gold medal hold. Johnson battled past two medalists from the World Championships, then defeated Soviet Rinvidas Bilus for the gold. Silver medalists Parker White and Romallis Ellis from the U.S., and Engels Pedroza from Venezuela, were the only other non-Soviet boxers to make the final round.

Even before the opening bell of the first bout, the U.S. Department of Defense dealt a telling blow to the U.S. boxing team. Invoking a little-known regulation, the Pentagon banned nine armed forces boxers, including three National Champions, from competing in the Soviet Union.

The last-minute replacements were virtually unknown, even to their coaches. Four of them – welterweight Ricky Royal, middleweight Lorenzo Wright, heavyweight Ike Padilla and light heavyweight Michael Simon – surprisingly made it to the semifinals. Each of the U.S. hopefuls, however, was unable to overcome the tremendous obstacles of little preparation, a hasty arrival and a powerful Soviet boxing machine. Seventeen year-old Simon of Washington, D.C. personified the plight of the eager, yet inexperienced, new contingent. Recruited only hours before the Opening Ceremony, the veteran of only 14 bouts nevertheless advanced to the semifinals. There he found himself in the ring against World Cup Champion Nurmagomed Shanovazov, who won a 5-0 decision and continued on to win the light heavyweight gold medal.

Even those U.S. boxers unaffected by the ban seemed demoralized and off-stride. Experienced and talented heavyweight Michael Bent, fresh from a bronze medal in the 1986 World Championships, carried the best hopes for American success. Bent, however, dropped a 4-1 decision in his second fight to last-minute Soviet substitute Vladimir Balay. Super heavyweight Kilbert Pierce faced the unenviable task of taking on World Cup Champion Vyachislav Yakovlev, the fighter who recently defeated Cuba's redoubtable Teofilo Stevenson. Yakovlev won a convincing decision on his way to the some more Soviet gold.

After their pummeling at the hands of the American team in Montreal in 1976, Soviet boxers abandoned their awkward stand-up style. During the Goodwill Games the Soviets gave notice – with 10 of 11 gold medals – that they are prepared to give the world's best boxers all they can handle.

Venezuela's Engels Pedroza, one of four non-Soviets to survive until the gold medal round, is safely beyond the reach of Soviet Igor Ruzhnikov in the light welterweight final.

U.S. silver medalist Parker White scores in the final round against Soviet Ruslan Taramov in their middleweight fight for the gold.

In featherweight action, Venezuela's Jose Luis Fernandez's punch leaves him open to the USSR's gold medalist "Samson" Kazarjan.

Soviet super heavyweight champion Aleksandr Miroshnichenko puts away Ali Ahmed Baluchi of Kuwait in their semi-final slugfest.

"Dance like a butterfly . . .".

Soviet Vyachislav Yakovlev and American Kilbert Pierce exchange blows in super heavyweight action.

Olympic gold medalist Steve Hegg pumps through in the men's 4km individual pursuit.

Cycling

The track inside Moscow's Olympic Velodrome is surfaced with wood from Siberian larch trees, making it one of the world's fastest. The forest surrounding the Olympic Velodrome is filled with Russian fir trees planted in honor of cycling champions and world record holders, making it one of the world's densest. Olympic Velodrome employees were kept busy cleaning the track and clearing the forest as three world records were shattered, eight new champions were crowned, and eleven Russian fir trees were planted during the three days of cycling competition.

The GDR's Michael Hubner ignited to a world mark of 10.24 seconds in the men's 200-meter flying start, breaking the five-year-old record of Soviet Sergei Kopylov by .005 seconds. In the women's 200-meter flying start, the USSR's Erika Salumiaee sped in under her own 1985 world record by .006 seconds as she clocked in at a blurring pace of 11.489 seconds. The Soviet 4,000-meter team pursuit squad outdid them both by breaking the world record twice: the first, an unofficial 4:12.84 in the qualifying heat; and the second, an indisputably official 4:12.41 in their gold-medal race past Czechoslovakia. Three of the four record-breaking Soviet team pursuit members also went on to sweep the 4,000-meter individual pursuit as Vyacheslav Ekimov (4:26.07), Gintautas Umaras (4:30.75) and Aleksandr Krasnov (4:30.91) cycled to the gold, silver and bronze medals.

Soviet Uldis Bremanis won the 1,000-meter time trials (1:03.566), falling one second short of the world record. His teammate Otar Mchedlishvili (1:04.583) took the silver, followed by GDR's Andreas Ganske. The Soviet victory streak continued in the 50-km. points race when silver medalist Ales Trcka of Czechoslovakia fell 29 points short of Soviet gold medalist Viktor Manakov, and Bulgaria's Stancho Stanchev took the bronze.

Sally Hodge of Great Britain (62 points) and Finland's Tea Vikstadt (29 points) succeeded in turning the tide of Soviet gold in the 20-km. points race as they outdistanced the 20-point total of the USSR's bronze medalist, Galina Supron. In the women's sprint, Erika Salumiaee added luster to her 200-meter flying start world record by garnering the gold in her finals victory over countrywoman and Goodwill Ambassador Galina Tsareva.

The race for the gold in the men's sprints featured a semifinal match-up of 1980 Olympic Champion Lutz Hesslich of the GDR against 1984 Olympic Champion Mark Gorski. As a result of an ankle injury, Gorski was not in top form. Hesslich, however, displayed the same form which has made him twice World Champion as he shut out the American, 2-0. Hesslich went on to defeat teammate and fierce rival Hubner for the gold, while Australia's Gary Niewand raced past Gorski for the bronze.

While Gorski was "on the mend," teammate Melinda Mayfield was on a tear in the women's 3,000-meter individual pursuit. In her first international competition, Mayfield came within 1.10 seconds of winning her gold-medal race against Switzerland's Barbara Ganz. "I've only been cycling for 14 months on the U.S. team, and I feel like now I've got the 'nerves out' in international competition" she said. What Mayfield did not explain was that she also got the "medal out," the only U.S. medal in this international competition. It represented a formidable beginning for the American who came within 1.10 seconds of being honored in the forest outside the velodrome with a fir tree of her own.

Sizing up the competition in the women's sprint.

An American rider "splits the wind" for her pursuing teammate.

Cat-and-mouse tactics are the rule in the sprint, as shown by GDR's Michael Hubner (left) and Lutz Hesslich (right).

Olympic silver medalist Nelson Vails began his career as a New York City bicycle courier.

The Soviets broke the world record twice in the team pursuit during the Goodwill Games competition.

Three world records were shattered and eight new champions were crowned on the Velodrome's fast Siberian larch track.

In their quest for the group points gold meda

American riders take a look at themselves on a LeRoy Neiman canvas.

clists line the track whose history boasts 116 world records.

Andezhela Statsylevich of the Soviet Union won the women's platform gold medal.

DIVING

When American diver Kent Ferguson walked into the Olympic Sports Complex, he had a premonition about the competition. Pointing to the divers from China and the USSR, he said, "They're going to be the toughest for us to beat."

Soviet diver Sergei Gurylev stood 33 feet above the shimmering pool, leading American Dan Watson by only 5.34 points before his next-to-last dive. Gurylev's feet left the platform. Gravity took charge, pulling him downward at 30 miles per hour. In 1½ seconds he completed a spectacularly clean inward 3½ somersaults in the tuck position. His 86.40 points, the single highest score in the competition, clinched the gold medal in his first international men's platform contest. Watson, in what may have been his last international event, before entering medical school, was only 5.31 points ahead of China's Feng Gao at the start of the final round. Scoring a strong 76.80 on his 1½ somersaults with 3½ twists, Watson ripped the water's surface for the silver.

Two days earlier, Kent Ferguson from Cedar Rapids, Iowa, approached his final dive from the springboard with a slim chance for a gold medal. Following Nikolai Drozhin, Ferguson needed a near-perfect 83.01 points to catch the Soviets' best diver. Despite the highest score of the evening, Ferguson fell three points short of Drozhin's gold-medal total. His stunning dive was more than enough, however, to raise the American's silver medal total above that of Chinese bronze medalist Delyand Li.

In the women's springboard, the GDR's Brita Baldus trailed China's Jiangin Li by 15 points at the beginning of the final round. When Li scored only 48.72 points on her final dive, Baldus edged past her breaking the Soviet lock on the diving gold. The Soviets salvaged the bronze medal when Zhanna Cirulnikova, after losing her final dive against American Tristan Baker, held on by .57 of a point.

Prior to her first attempt in the women's platform competition, America's best, Michele Mitchell, tried to settle her nerves. "When I get too tense," she said, "I just remind myself that there are billions of people who could care less about my diving." Perhaps, but diving aficionados the world over watched in awe while platform divers Andezhela Statsylevich and Olga Blinova (USSR) and Mitchell, treated them to repeated displays of elegant beauty. Respectively, they garnered gold, silver and bronze medals.

At the end of the competition, Ferguson and Watson left with smiles on their faces and silver medals in their hands. Both were grateful that Ferguson's premonition, while right in describing the competition, was only half right when it came to awarding the medals.

American Dan Watson acknowledges the crowd's warm applause.

"Gravity took charge, pulling Gurylev downward at 30 miles per hour."

American bronze medalist Michele Mitchell treated the crowd to repeated displays of elegant beauty.

Platform gold medalist Sergei Gurylev of the Soviet Union.

Soviet world pairs champions Ekaterina Gordeeva and Sergei Grinkov soared across the ice to "Fly Dove, Fly."

FIGURE SKATING

"An exhibition – no judging, no medals; just the best skaters in the world having fun." That's how TBS commentators Curt Gowdy and Peggy Fleming described the Goodwill Games skating exhibition at the Lenin Stadium Palace of Sports. How did the skaters feel about it?

"It was the most exciting thing I've ever done," raved 1986 World Champion Debi Thomas after she and Soviet Vladimir Kotin paired up for a heart-throbbing ice-dance rendition of Michael Jackson's "Billie Jean." Thomas went on to exclaim, "They were totally excited. . . This is something the crowd has never seen." In fact, it was something no one had ever seen – two skaters from different countries performing together as ice-dancing partners in a major international skating event. For a full ninety seconds, an over-flowing international crowd was unified by a shared love of music, sport and the two young skaters on the ice.

Two nights of skating exhibitions by forty premier skaters from the USSR and the USA had prepared the audience for its love affair with Thomas and Kotin. The exhibition encouraged a degree of creativity usually unseen in more formal competitions.

Many of the performers enhanced their routines with a blending of skating and musical styles from East and West. Soviet world pairs champions Ekaterina Gordeeva and Sergei Grinkov soared across the ice to "Fly Dove, Fly," while another Soviet duo, Natalya Annenko and Genrikh Stretensy, pranced to "Putting on the Ritz" and glided to Gershwin's "Summertime."

Men's World Champion Brian Boitano (USA) opened his routine by bringing America's "Wild West" to Moscow, high-stepping to a cowboy medley. Boitano then saluted his appreciative hosts with a rousing finale to the Russian folk song "Kamarinskaya." America's Tiffany Chin delighted the audience with her interpretation of "Chasing Rainbows," and Scott Williams brought down the house with his rock 'n roll rendition of "Elvis and his greatest hits."

Two evenings of such creative performances set the stage for Kotin to beckon Thomas to be his skating partner. At the close of their history-making routine, Thomas was asked through an interpreter her reaction to the two nights of skating exhibitions. Her response of "Totally awesome" left the interpreter with a blank stare on his face, but Debi was easily understood by the audience, still on its feet applauding.

The USSR's world class ice-dancing duo Natalia Annenko and Genrich Stretensky.

Soviet Vladimir Kotin and American Debi Thomas end their routine amidst waves of applause and showers of bouquets.

American ice-dancing duo
Scott Gregory and Suzanne Semanick

The World Champion ice-dancing team of Natalia Bestemianova and Andrei Bukin.

*World Championship
bronze medalist
Tiffany Chin.*

The finale

USA pairs Peter Oppegard and Jill Watson

Valentin Mogilny demonstrates the strength which made him champion of the pommel horse.

GYMNASTICS

"In the Soviet Union there is only one privileged class – the children," Vladimir Lenin once said. The thousands of young Soviet gymnasts who inspired the world during the Opening Ceremony had given ample warning of what was to be confirmed at the Goodwill Games artistic and rhythmic gymnastics competitions – Soviet children repay their privilege with diligent hard work in the arena of sport.

The dedication of the young Soviet artistic gymnasts resulted in an amazing sweep of the gold medals in the team and individual competitions. Not since the glory days of Nikolai Andreonov, Lyudmilla Tourischeva, Nelli Kim and Olga Korbut had the Soviet Union dominated an international gymnastics competition so completely as it did in the Goodwill Games. Time and again, Yuri Korolev and Elena Shushunova stood atop the winners' stand to hear the Soviet national anthem and receive their gold medals.

Korolev began his heroics by leading the Soviets to the team title with wins on the rings and the horizontal bars. He completed his medal assault by capturing the gold for the all-around men's title. In the women's all-around competition, Shushunova was edged out by teammate Vera Kolesnikova by .15 of a point, but claimed gold on the vault, beam, and floor exercise. She polished off the uneven bars with a perfect 10. With a breathtaking display of strength and control in every exercise, Korolev and Shushunova set the standards for the competition. Most all of the best gymnasts were present, but the teams from Bulgaria (men's silver), GDR (women's silver), China (men's and women's bronze), Japan, USA and Romania became little more than spectators of the Soviets' magnificence. Joyce Wilborn of Willingboro, New Jersey found herself in an elite group of ten other non-Soviet winners as she captured America's only medal, a bronze in the vault.

Seventeen-year-old Soviet rhythmic gymnast Tatyana Druchinina wrote her own chapter of sports history at the Goodwill Games. Quietly and without fanfare, she scored perfect marks of 10.00 with three of the four pieces of apparatus to capture the all-around title. Her teammates, Marina Lobach and Galina Beloglazova, were nearly as perfect, each turning in three 10.00 performances for the silver and bronze, respectively.

Only the GDR's Bianka Dittrich could interrupt the Soviets' gold medal run, as she performed flawlessly to share the gold with Druchinina and Lobach in the rope event. At the competition's conclusion, U.S. women's artistic coach Don Peters was left to wonder aloud if the rest of the world's gymnasts could ever rise to compete evenly with the privileged young Soviets, who communicated an abiding love of their sport with every movement.

Ball competition in Rhythmic Gymnastics.

Tatyana Druchinina (USSR) scored perfect marks of 10.00 on three of the four individual apparatus, capturing the all-around title.

Elena Shushunova (USSR), heir presumptive to
Olga Korbut and Nadia Comaneci, performs
on the uneven bars.

Yuri Korolev (USSR) took the honors
in the men's individual all-around
competition. He ties with four others
as the world's top-ranking gymnast.

America's Joyce Wilborn displays her strength and flexibility on the beam.

Olympic team gold medalist Timothy Daggett of the United States competes on the parallel bars.

Elena Shushunova (USSR) polishes off a perfect 10 with her dismount from the uneven bars.

Luming Fu of China shows his prowess on the rings.

Jennifer Sey (USA), coming back from a serious leg injury, competes in the floor exercise.

Jana Vogel (GDR) defies gravity on the balance beam.

Tiny Kim Gy Mok (China) delighted the crowds with her spunk and determination.

The calm face of China's Li Chungang belies the strain as he flexes to an iron cross.

Leora "Sam" Jones was the second leading scorer of the women's competition, amassing 31 goals for the American team.

HANDBALL (Team)

It seemed somehow appropriate that, from a new and emerging international sporting event, a young, unknown Soviet athlete and an unheralded American team would emerge as major stories. Their stories unfolded during the team handball competition at the Dynamo Palace of Sport.

It was a surprise to no one when the Soviet men won the gold medal in team handball, but that they were led in scoring by a secret weapon in the form of 6' 9" Aleksandr Tuchkin was nothing short of astonishing. Equally astonishing, Tuchkin's most memorable moment came in a medal-deciding contest against the U.S team which had never won a medal in major international competition.

The drama for the America team had developed at the very start of the round-robin tournament. With 11:20 remaining in the U.S. team's opening game, a Czech goal and a penalty shot cut the U.S. margin to one. Joe Story and Steve Goss responded with scores to make it 22-19, with 4:37 left to play. Repeated saves by goalie Bill Kessler held off the Czechs until Goss finally put it away with a score in the last thirty seconds. The 23-21 U.S. win was its first ever over Czechoslovakia.

Against Iceland in the second round, the U.S. again found its lead dwindling in the final minutes. This time it was Bob Djokovich and Jim Buehning whose late goals preserved a 22-19 win, advancing the U.S. to a showdown with Tuchkin and his Soviet teammates.

Tuchkin wasted no time in introducing himself to his American opponents. During the first seven minutes of the game the young Soviet scored four of his team's first five goals to open up a 5-2 Soviet lead. With four minutes left in the game the Soviet lead had grown even greater, 22-16. A Buehning goal, followed with two more by Joe McVein, brought the U.S. within three to make things interesting. Interesting it was, particularly for Tuchkin, who celebrated his 21st birthday by scoring his tenth and the game's final goal, for a 23-19 win.

Three days later the gold-medal Soviets completed their tournament sweep by routing Poland, 26-18. Their victory relegated the Poles to a bronze medal and secured a cherished silver for the U.S.

In the women's competition, the USSR's Natalia Kirchik led all scorers and also led her team to a 26-20 gold medal victory over France.

Leora "Sam" Jones was America's bright spot, finishing just two goals behind Linchuk in the scoring race. But even Jones' 31 goals could not offset the absence of her team's top two goalies, who were kept from competing by the U.S. Defense Department. Also absent was injured mainstay Cindy Springer, leaving the high-scoring Jones to conclude, "With those three, we were in contention for the gold. Without them, we went zero and five. It's that simple."

Despite her team's misfortunes, the individual greatness of the American star was rewarded with a rose by the Soviet star, Tuchkin. Jones responded with a birthday kiss, providing the young Soviet yet another memorable moment in his encounter with the Americans.

Rosa Toth urges Hungary on toward the bronze medal.

Aleksandr Tuchkin, the Soviet secret weapon, gives himself a fitting 21st birthday gift as he scores one of his ten goals during this match against the USA.

The American handball team takes time out from the competition to pose in Red Square with a Russian dancing troupe.

Spectacular shots and daring plays led the Soviets to the gold.

Poland's Krzystof Szargiej scores a goal after Geir Svensson (6) and Tortergur Adalsteinsson (10) from Iceland fail to block it.

Natalia Kirchik (USSR), leading scorer of the tournament with 33 goals, fires another one during the match against the Americans.

A dancing Icelandic goalie blocks American Joe McVein's attempted goal.

An exhibition of drama and style in the men's epee.

MODERN PENTATHLON

In the Napoleonic era, a courier would wait outside the general's tent for urgent messages. When one was brought out, he mounted an unfamiliar horse and galloped off, leaping any obstacles in his path. Through enemy territory he fought his way with sword and pistol, swimming any rivers which barred his progress. When his horse gave out, he ran the rest of the way to complete his mission. Modern Pentathlon is a sport derived from the diverse skills used by these couriers. While the present day obstacles may not be so treacherous, they certainly are as rigorous.

The Soviet men totally dominated the five-day competition, easily taking the team gold and the top eight places of the individual standings. Vakhtang Yagorashvili emerged with 5,680 points and the individual gold medal, after overcoming a 12-second deficit to defeat teammate German Joferov in the cross-country run.

The U.S. men finished fourth, behind the Polish and Hungarian teams. The Americans' medal chances were dashed when former national champion and Army Captain Mike Burley was barred by the U.S. Defense Department ruling which prohibited its employees from competing. But Lori Norwood salvaged American pride and delivered the message that the U.S. would not be denied a medal finish. Starting the cross-country run in seventh place, Norwood edged Poland's Barbara Kotoska by 42 points to win the bronze. She thus became the first American woman to win a medal in international Modern Pentathlon competition.

Despite the strength of Norwood's finish, U.S. women competitors bowed to the grace and strength of the USSR's Tatyana Chernetskaya, who powered to 5,280 points and the gold — 48 points ahead of Sophie Moressee, the French silver medalist. But Chernetskaya's stellar individual performance was not enough to keep the deep Polish squad from capturing the team gold. The Soviets took the silver and the FRG the bronze.

Perhaps the men's and women's "Athlete of the Year" titles for 1986 should be awarded to Vakhtang Yagorashvilli and Tatyana Chernetskaya who rode, fenced, shot, swam and ran to the Goodwill Games gold medals. Modern Pentathlon was designed to challenge the world's most complete athlete. These two Soviet stars would have made admirable couriers in Napoleon's day.

Mexico's Jorge Garcia clears a jump.

Soviet spectators enjoy the women's cross-country run.

Pounding along on the cross country run are FRG's Frauke Holebein (10) and Sabine Krapf (11) and Sophie Moressee (9) of France.

A rider clears the first of many obstacles in the equestrian portion of Modern Pentathlon.

The 400m swim is one of the five events for men.

Emil Dimitrov of Bulgaria crosses the finish line.

Lori Norwood, the first American woman to win a medal in international Modern Pentathlon competition concentrates as she awaits her turn to shoot.

Viktor Kirienko (USSR) tied with four of his countrymen in the individual shooting competition.

Welcome to the world of motoball!

MOTOBALL

In an American television debut of the sport, the Soviet motoball team smothered FRG star Uwe Scheckenbecker with double coverage, and wheeled and kicked its way to 7-3 and 5-2 exhibition victories over the European All-Stars. Demonstrating Soviet hospitality, caviar was served at half time. Welcome to the world of motoball!

Four motorcycle-riding players kick a beach-size ball in this unique blend of motocross and soccer. An unmounted goalie is permitted to play the ball with his hands. "Players occasionally break legs, but not often," said Boris Loganov, Chairman of the Soviet Motoball Commission. "It is the goalies who get injured more because of powerful shots and a heavy ball. Sometimes they break their hands."

The Soviet ace, 44-year-old Vladimir Serebriakov, led his team with three goals. He demonstrated the same skills for which a gifted soccer player is praised – the finesse to weave the ball down the field, accuracy in passing and shooting, and tenacity on defense – all the while perched precariously atop a speeding 250 cc motorcycle.

Fresh from their fourteenth European Cup Championship, Soviets Alexander Tzarev, Sergei Chasoskih and Serebriakov displayed amazing dexterity by controlling the ball with their feet and the wheels of their bikes, avoiding tackles to out-manuever and out-class their European opponents.

Soviet superiority in international motoball, which is also played in 11 European countries and Canada, is supported by some 5,000 players and more than 200 teams which are divided into major and minor leagues. A motoball factory in Kovrov does nothing but build motorcycles for motoball.

For the Soviet faithful who jammed the stadium outside of Moscow, cheering their team to victory had long since become a tradition. Novice American spectators like TBS' Skip Caray were fascinated immediately. "I've never seen a motoball game I didn't like," quipped Caray. Caviar in the Astrodome, anyone?

Caviar accompanied the half time dancing.

"Sometimes the goalies break their hands."

Soviet ace Vladimir Serebriakov weaves the ball down field.

The FRG's Uwe Scheckenbecker maneuvers for a score against a Soviet defense of boots and bikes.

Kim Santiago, coxswain of the U.S. women's eights, scrutinizes the course ahead as she prepares to lead her crewmates.

ROWING

In his blue sailing cap and sunglasses, unrecognized by most of the rowing competition spectators, sat Ted Turner. Remaining long after the competition ended, Turner watched as Soviet and American rowers gathered at the side of the canal to trade jerseys and crew stories. In one swift motion, Turner responded to their camaraderie and the dramatic competition it had followed. Thumbs up!

The ecstasy of victory was in the voice of American stroke Andy Sudduth. "It's so exhilarating to move through another crew and win in the last possible second," he exulted. In the final event of the day, Sudduth and his men's eights crew mates rowed a powerful final 500 meters to pass the Soviet crew, taking the gold by three-quarters of a length.

The closeness of their race had proven to be the rule rather than the exception throughout the dual competition. In the women's four with coxswain, the Americans pulled even with the Soviets at the 1,500 meter mark but were unable to close, falling short at the finish by less than a boat length. After a troublesome start which left them three seconds behind at the 500 meter mark, the U.S. men's four with cox managed to come within a boat length of victory. Equally close were Americans Michael Teti and John Strotbeck in the pairs without cox, who lost to Soviet brothers Yuri and Nikolai Pimenov by less than 2½ seconds.

Narrow and thrilling Soviet victories continued until America's Angie Herron broke the USSR's streak by taking the gold in the women's lightweight singles. Her victory set the stage for Sudduth and his crew's exhilarating final win.

The fierceness of the competition was matched by the camaraderie at the finish. Just before returning their shells to the boathouse, the Soviet and American bow fours, who had just done battle in the last race, exchanged places. Stroking in unison down the canal, combined teams of blue-shirted Americans and red-shirted Soviets left Turner and the crowd on shore with a colorful memory of athletic unity.

The Soviet women's eights skims down the canal on the outskirts of Moscow.

Jonathan Smith of the U.S. men's four without cox cools off after a tiring battle with the Soviets.

Americans pull fiercely toward their common goal in the men's fours championship.

The U.S. men's eights team heaves a weary sigh of satisfaction after capturing the gold medal.

Soviet women relax after stroking their way to victory in the quads.

Brian Benz (USA) attempts to pick up the pace in lightweight single sculls action.

Ambidextrous American Luke Jensen doubled with teammate Pearce for the bronze.

TENNIS

Sheets of blowing rain covered the courts in the coastal city of Yurmula, where 64 players from 16 countries sought refuge inside the Daygava Tennis Complex to rally for the tennis gold. But neither wind nor rain nor change of venue could keep Caroline Kuhlman and Beverly Bowes from an all-American gold medal match-up in the women's singles competition.

Proving why they are two of the top-ranked amateur players in the U.S., the number one players from the Universities of Texas and Southern California dropped only one set each as they stormed to the finals. For Californian, Caroline Kuhlman, it made little difference that she was playing on the Baltic Sea rather than on the Pacific coast. She added to her 25-0 regular season collegiate winning streak by downing a determined Beverly Bowes in straight sets, 6-4, 7-5, to bring the gold medal a bit further west than Bowes had in mind.

In the women's doubles competition, Soviets Larisa Savchenko and Svetlana Parkhomenko, who had been singularly rejected earlier, overwhelmed Czechoslovakia's Iva Budarova and Marcella Skuherska in straight sets, 6-3, 6-3, to keep the gold a little further east than the Czechs would have liked. The Soviet duo's victory was not surprising; the two had twice defeated doubles teams featuring Chris Evert Lloyd in previous international play.

The men's singles gold medal stayed in the USSR when Andrei Chesnokov, quarterfinalist at the 1985 French Open, defeated Marian Vajda from Czechoslovakia. Americans Jay Berger and Brad Pearce had struggled valiantly, but Berger succumbed to Vajda in the quarterfinals, while Pearce managed to rally for the bronze.

In the men's doubles competition there was another all-American final, this one with the bronze medal at stake. Americans Brad Pearce and Luke Jensen traded the first four sets with teammates Jay Berger and Kelly Jones before taking the fifth set, 6-4. The gold was won by the USSR's Sergei Leonyuk and Aleksandr Zverev. After they were down two sets to one, they rallied past Czechoslovakians Karel Novacek and Vajda to take the final sets, 6-3, 6-3.

That the amateur Americans fared as well as they did against the experienced Eastern Europeans was impressive. As a result of their performance, the winds coming in from the Baltic Sea seemed a little less chilling for the U.S. collegians, and the future for U.S. tennis looks considerably brighter.

USC's Caroline Kuhlman captured the gold for the USA.

Czechoslovakia's Marian Vajda was the silver medal winner in the men's singles competition.

Left: American Brad Pearce won bronze medals in the men's singles and doubles competitions. Right: Andrei Chesnokov of the Soviet Union volleyed to victory in the men's singles.

Silver medalist Beverly Bowes is one of the top-ranked amateur players in the United States.

America's Pearce and Jensen with their Soviet fans.

141

The Soviets announce their comeback and go on to capture the gold.

VOLLEYBALL

A partisan crowd packed the Lenin Central Stadium Small Arena and watched nervously as a surprising French men's volleyball team threatened to keep the powerful Soviets from facing off with the Americans for the gold medal. The French succeeded in taking the Soviets to a final and deciding game, but the dream USA – USSR match-up was meant to be.

On the heels of the Olympic gold in Los Angeles and the 1985 World Cup Championship, a veteran U.S. men's volleyball team arrived in Moscow anticipating the contest with the Soviets for the gold. Despite America winning seven of eight games against the Soviets during the preceding year, six-year American stalwart Dusty Dvorak appeared to have a premonition of what was in store for his team in Moscow when he said, "You can't talk U.S. dominance because, until this year, the Soviets have always been the best."

Dominance appeared to be close at hand for the Americans when they reached match-point in the fourth game of the dream match. Even harder pressed to reach the gold medal match, the Soviet squad seemed to forget the leaden legs earned in its exhausting victory over the French, and turned back the Americans at the brink of defeat. Unwilling to relinquish world superiority, the Soviets turned to consoling the crestfallen Americans after defeating them in a grueling five-game match.

Earlier in the Games, the U.S. women, whose team had been completely rebuilt after winning an Olympic silver in 1984, appeared to be out of the medal chase after losing their first two matches to the People's Republic of Korea and Japan. A 3-1 victory over Czechoslovakia put them in a tie with the PRK team and qualified them for the semifinals on a technicality – they had won more games than the PRK.

Though the Soviet women handled the Americans 3-1 in their semifinal match – and went on to win the gold by defeating Peru – the young American team rebounded against the Japanese with a masterful 3-0 shutout for the bronze medal.

In the men's bronze-medal game, the French team, exhausted by its emotional losses to the Soviets and the Americans, fell to the Japanese. As a result of their surprisingly strong start, however, the French men came away from Moscow displaying signs of future greatness.

Steve Timmons (USA), known as "Red," serves against the French.

Karch Kiraly (USA-15) powers the ball past Alain Fabiani (France-12).

French player Eric Bouvier is stunned after suffering a 3-1 loss to the Americans.

Ute Oldenburg (9) of the German Democratic Republic sets the ball for teammate Djorte Schtjudmann (10).

The Soviet Union returns a shot against Peru in the gold medal match.

U.S. women players are congratulated after wrestling the bronze medal from Japan in a three-game sweep.

Peru's Natalia Malaga digs out a spike against the Soviets during the championship match.

An imposing wall of arms
is formed by Dusty Dvorak,
Doug Partie, and Karch Kiraly.

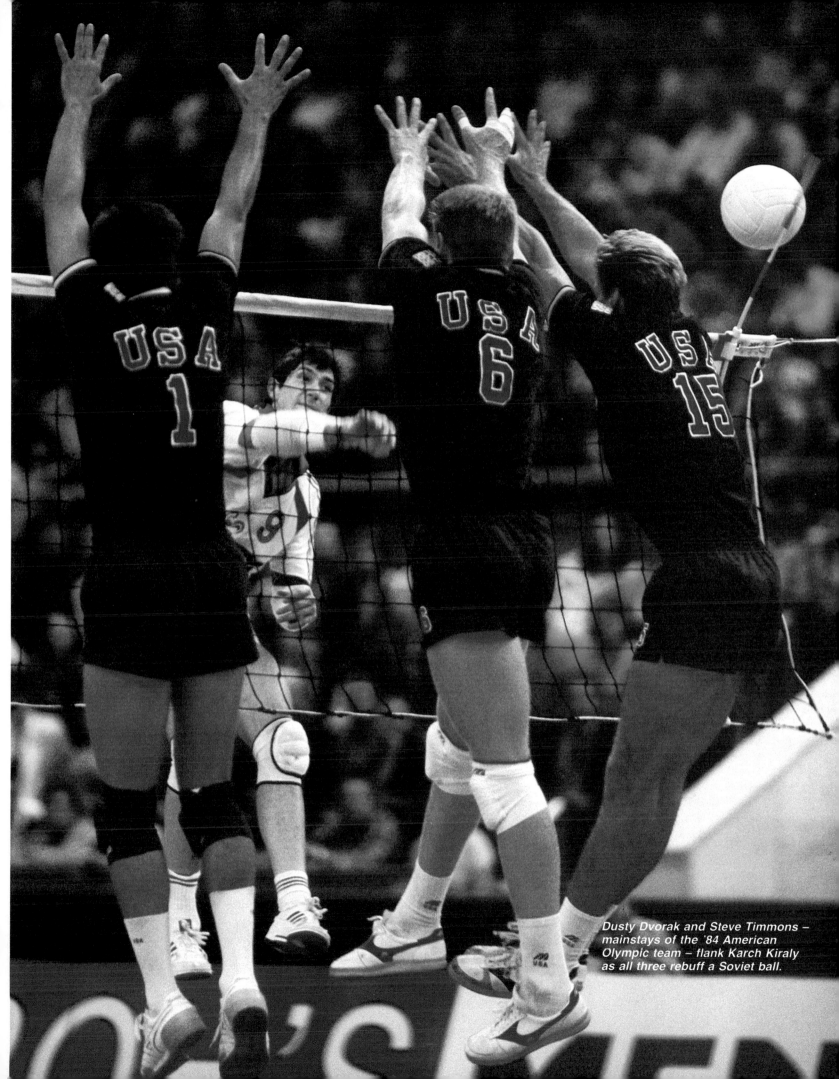

Dusty Dvorak and Steve Timmons — mainstays of the '84 American Olympic team — flank Karch Kiraly as all three rebuff a Soviet ball.

Arpad Gaspar of Hungary poses for a pass as Jody Campbell of the U.S. closes in. The Americans tied the game during the last seven seconds of this sizzling match.

WATER POLO

Both the Soviet and American water polo teams had to survive a tough Hungarian team in order to compete for the gold medal. In a brutal match marked by 20 ejections, the Soviets narrowly defeated Hungary, 7-5. Against the U.S., the Hungarians led 8-7 until the last seven seconds when American Mike Evans' corner shot salvaged a tie and set the stage for a USA – USSR gold-medal final.

The good news for the U.S. water polo team members was that they out-scored the Soviets 5-4 in the second half of the match for the gold; the bad news was that they lost the first half, 6-0. "It was really bad out there," said U.S. team captain Terry Schroeder, probably not at all certain whether he was describing the cold, drizzling rain which fell throughout, or his team's first-half shooting touch.

Only 31 seconds had elapsed when America's Alan Mouchawar missed what for him should have been an automatic four-meter penalty shot. Ninety-one seconds later the Soviets' Sergei Naumov broke away for a solo slam over U.S. goalie Craig Wilson, which was followed a minute later by a power-play goal by the USSR's Evgeni Grishin. Mouchawar's near-miss was as close as the Americans would come in the first half, and Naumov's second goal with 35 seconds remaining capped a six-goal Soviet onslaught.

While the weather didn't change in the second half, the American shooting touch did. Third-quarter goals by Jeff Campbell and James Bergeson, and two goals by Mouchawar and one by Evans in the fourth, brought respect to the U.S. effort.

After his team's 10-5 victory, Soviet coach Boris Popov offered a forecast for his seasoned team. "The tradition has been continued today and we have no intention of abandoning it," he said, referring to Soviet strength in Olympic and World Championship play. In from the rain, America's Schroeder had a forecast of his own. "We have only six Olympians back from our '84 silver medal team whose average age was about 27. . . The average age of this team is 23. . . In a year, we'll be right up there."

American team captain Terry Schroeder finds himself caught in the grasp of Viktor Berendyuga. The Soviets won 10-5 and claimed the gold.

U.S. goalie Craig Wilson explodes from the water in defense of his territory.

Terry Schroeder holds off Holland's Wico DeVries prior to scoring 3 goals in a 12-5 U.S. victory.

Leonid Taranenko, (USSR), world record holder in the 110+ kg. braces for the final phase of his lift.

WEIGHTLIFTING

In the 1948 Olympics in London, U.S. weightlifters won four of six gold medals and one bronze medal. The USSR won none. In the 1976 Olympics in Montreal, U.S. weightlifters won one silver medal. The USSR won a single silver medal as well; they also won seven of the nine gold medals, and the name of super heavyweight Vasily Alexeev reached household acclaim. Nothing changed but the names – Alexeev, Kolesnikov, and Zaitsev were replaced by Balzev, Zakharevich and Taranenko – as the Soviets continued their awesome forty-year assault on weightlifting gold.

Ruslan Balaev instigated the Soviet attack in his tight battle for the top prize in the 100 kg. division. After taking a second place finish in the snatch to Romania's Nicu Vlad, who won the event with a lift of 187.5 kg. (413¼ lbs.), the fiercely determined Balaev responded with a clean and jerk of 227.5 kg. (501½ lbs.). He edged Vlad by less than five pounds to an overall gold medal total of 412.5 kg. (909¼ lbs.), the first of many confirmations of Soviet weightlifting supremacy.

World Champion Yuri Zakharevich protected his 110 kg. title by outlifting Czechoslovakia's Anton Baraniak. Zakharvich bettered the Czech by 11 lbs. in each category, and his overall total of 417.5 kg. (920¼ lbs.) left him only eleven pounds shy of his own world record.

Soviet Leonid Taranenko, Olympic recordholder in the clean and jerk, 110 kg. category, moved up a notch to power for three gold medals in 110 + kg. division. Taranenko's gold medal total of 447.5 kg. (986½ lbs.) was particularly impressive since he defeated compatriot and 1985 World Championship silver medalist Alexsandr Gunjashev by 12.5 kg. (27½ lbs.)

The Izmailovo Sports Palace, the site of the Soviet gold medal sweep, was described by Weightlifting Federation President Gottfried Schoedl as a "model design." It provides a perfect home for a Soviet weightlifting program modelled after a forty-year plan of international success and prosperity.

America's Rich Schutz musters all of his strength in the snatch, 100 kg. division.

Soviet Ruslan Balaev won overall honors by a thin margin in the 100 kg. division.

The pit crew considers a weighty problem.

Yuri Dandik lifts to a 100 kg bronze medal in the clean and jerk.

The skills of U.S. champion Dave Schultz are sorely tried as he attempts to pin Adlan Varaev of the USSR.

WRESTLING

The Druzhba Sports Hall was the stage for a Cinderella story in the making as a young, aggressive Bulgarian team grappled its way to the gold medal final. With four Junior World Champions in their midst, the Bulgarians surprised the U.S. with a 5-5 tie and thrashed Turkey 8-2. Waiting for the would-be Cinderella team were the World Champion Soviets, with a stage script of their own.

S oviet Arsen Fadzaev (68 kg.) needed only a cameo appearance to play the leading role in the finals of the team competition – he pinned Bulgaria's Anguel Sirakov in only 52 seconds. While the rest of the Soviet performance was not quite so dramatic, it was undeniably impressive as the Soviets recorded three superior decisions to win every match. Their gold medal victory was an appropriate encore to their earlier 10-0 shutouts of Japan and Mongolia.

Disappointed by not reaching the team finals, six U.S. wrestlers joined three Bulgarians and one Turk in the gold medal finals of the individual competition. Again, ten Soviet wrestlers were waiting to meet this new group of gold medal hopefuls. Of these hopefuls, only three could slightly revise a script which called for another story of Soviet dominance.

John Smith of the U.S. was the first to defeat a Soviet wrestler in the Goodwill Games. Smith (62 kg.) ended a 33-match Soviet winning streak with a 6-3 decision over Khazer Isaev.

America's 1984 Olympic Champion Dave Schultz (74 kg.) added another gold to his collection by winning 4-2 over Soviet Adlan Varaev. In victory, Schultz dramatically held his three-month-old son, Alexander, aloft, exclaiming, "I always like it when I win, especially here."

In the heavyweight division, '84 Olympic gold medalist Bruce Baumgartner of the U.S. faced '85 World Champion David Gobedzhishvili of the Soviet Union. The two giants of freestyle wrestling had split in their previous four meetings, but in the final seconds of their rubber match, Baumgartner came back to defeat the Soviet on criteria for the third American gold medal.

Although the Soviets "curtain call" in the individual competition was slightly less praiseworthy than their performance in the team competition, the Soviets won seven of ten individual golds, compiling a closing night composite 37-3 record.

A boisterous Turkish crowd cheered their wrestlers on to silver and bronze medals.

Kevin Darkus (USA) scores on an escape from Niamdavagiyn Ganbaatar (Mongolia) on his way to a 5-0 win in the team competition.

Andre Metzge strengthens America's grasp on the team bronze against Mongolia's Nyamdvagiyn Ganbaatar.

Eyes locked in combat, gold medalist Bruce Baumgartner (USA) and world champion David Gobedzhishivili (USSR) battle it out for the individual super-heavyweight gold medal.

The U.S. wrestling team eventually came out on top of the Mongolian team by capturing the Bronze.

USSR's Georgi Shaiduko on a spinnaker
reach. He shared the Soling Class gold
with America's John Kostecki.

YACHTING

Near the charming medieval town of Tallinn, the competition was fierce for the yachting gold medals in seven classes. Heavy winds blowing in from the Baltic Sea would greatly affect the spirits and the strategies of 124 sailors from 26 countries who came to race on the Gulf of Finland.

Gusty winds on the opening day of competition raised the hopes of Americans Skip Elliott (Tornado) and Gerald Braun (Flying Dutchman) as they led their respective fleets across the finish. But as the winds died, Soviets Yuri Konovalov (Tornado) and Aleksandr Shpilko (Flying Dutchman) found the calmer conditions to their advantage, and they swept the U.S. favorites in the final five races for the gold medals.

Fortunately for America's 5 ft., 100 lbs. Kathy Steele (Sailboard), the initial winds forced a one-day postponement of her match-up with Poland's 5 ft. 8 in., 143 lbs. Joanna Buzinska. Steele's prayers for lighter winds were answered for five of the six races, and she tied Buzinska for the gold. Ironically, Steele's teammate in the men's Sailboard class, Mike Gebhardt, missed his chance for the gold when the final race was cancelled due to *no* wind. Gebhardt finished with the silver, between the USSR's gold medalist, Yevgeni Bogatyryov, and Holland's bronze medalist, Marcel Reitsema.

After the first four races in the Star class, Soviets Guram Biganishvili and Aleksandr Zubin trailed Americans Mark Reynolds and Henry Sprague. In the fourth race it was Reynolds' error, not the wind, which aided his competitors. The American skipper misjudged the finish line and, instead of heading toward the committee boat which was favored, he continued on toward the outer distance mark only to watch the Soviets cross the line first. But Reynolds' error proved not to be a costly one, since he and Sprague swept the final two races to win the gold medal.

Canadians Karen and Gail Johnson sailed to victories in the first three races of the women's 470 class, holding off Americans Pease Herndon and Cindy Goff, who took the silver medal. In the men's 470, America's Morgan Reeser and Kevin Burnham came back after a fifteenth-place finish in the first race to win three out of the next six, finishing ahead of the German Democratic Republic and Canada.

Gyorgi Shaiduko of the USSR won three races in the Soling competition, while Hungary's Gyorgi Finasi led his crew to victory in another. But neither could better the American crew of John Kostecki, Bob Billingham and Will Bayliss, who took the gold. Kostecki seemed to almost apologize for his team's victory by saying, "Shaiduko beat us four times out of seven. . . he deserves to win."

In the Finn class, there was never any doubt about which boat deserved to win when Soviet Oleg Khopyorsky left the fleet in his wake in six of the seven races. Greatly impressed with Khoperskij's sailing strategies, the American team invited Khoperskij to America in hopes that other U.S. sailors can learn something from him. Their invitation demonstrated a spirit over which the wind from the Baltic Sea had no effect.

A Tornado hard on the wind.

Pease Herndon and Cindy Goff, U.S. silver medalists, cross the German Democratic Republic and Hungarian 470's.

The gate from the upper city to the lower city in ancient Tallinn.

USSR's Oleg Khopyorsky won a perfect score in the Finn Class.

A fleet of diaphanous wings crowds across the start line.

Like a colorful butterfly, Kathy Steele works her way up the last windward leg on her way to the gold she shared with Poland's Joanna Buzinska.

The yachting competition opened with colorful festivities.

Gerald Braun and Bill Kenney (USA), Flying Dutchman silver medalists, hoist the spinnaker as they round the windward mark.

John Kostecki (USA) on his way to the leeward mark and the Soling gold.

Down goes Grigori Verichev (703) of the Soviet Union.

JUDO

It was fitting that the final event in the 1986 Goodwill Games was judo, a sport which derives from an ancient weaponless form of self-defense. The sport teaches that "soft prevails over hard" and that a defender "conquers by yielding," appropriate lessons with which to conclude these games of goodwill.

Seven Soviet judokas nearly monopolized the gold-medal platform for their homeland during the eight-event competition. Khabil Biktashev of the Soviet Union, a bronze medalist in the 1985 World Championships, won the final Goodwill Games gold medal in the open class. Bitktashev never had to face Czechoslovakian Jiri Sosna (fifth in the World Championships), or Dmitri Zapryanov of Bulgaria (bronze at the 1985 championships in the heavyweight division), who both lost early contests.

American heavyweight Steve Cohen split matches with two 1985 bronze medalists on his way to the silver, the only medal won by an American. Narrowly defeating the Bulgarian, Zapryanov, Cohen then lost a close match for the gold to Grigori Verichev of the Soviet Union. Cohen was one of the three American judokas affected by the U.S. boycott of the 1980 Olympics in Moscow, making his 1986 Moscow success particularly gratifying. He won the applause of the 3,000-strong crowd when he warmly embraced Verichev on the winners' podium. "This is my first big international competition and I am just really pleased to be here," exclaimed Cohen.

The Soviet Union's unheralded Viktor Poddubny prevailed in the half-heavyweight class, one of the toughest in the competition. Neither the GDR's Andreas Preschel (1983 World Champion), Douglas Viera of Brazil (1984 Olympic silver medal), nor America's Bob Berland (1984 Olympic silver in the middleweight class) were able to prevent Viktor Poddubryi from capturing the gold medal.

The lone non-Soviet gold medalist was Mikihiro Mukai of Japan, who captured the gold in the extra-lightweight division on the closing day of the Games. Although his country was the birthplace of modern judo, and his team took four gold medals in the 1985 World Championships, no one could match the seven Soviet judokas in this competition.

Heavyweight Steve Cohen took the silver, the only medal won by an American.

A Soviet judoka resists.

Andreas Prescel (610) of the German Democratic Republic.

Hungary's Laszlo Tolnai (704) grapples with Aleksandr Tarasov (712) of the Soviet Union.

Apollo astronaut Thomas Stafford joins Jane Smith beside a photographic tribute to her daughter, Samantha.

Jeremy Gall
St. Peters School
Torrington, Connecticut   11 Years Old

Gregory Dean
Mt. Blue Junior High School
Farmington, Maine   14 Years Old

Amy Lester
Cuba Central School
Cuba, New York   13 Years Old

"I chose this topic because I like sports and hope that these games will truly bridge the gap between our two great nations."

"If we all work together everyone wins."

"The bear is the children trying to bring the world together in peace."

174

"In The Spirit Of Goodwill"

Mr. Yuri Andropov
The Kremlin
Moscow, USSR

Dear Mr. Andropov,

My name is Samantha Smith. I am ten years old. Congratulations on your new job. I have been worrying about Russia and the United States getting into a nuclear war. Are you going to vote to have a war or not? If you aren't please tell me how you are going to help not have a war. This question you do not have to answer, but I would like to know why you want to conquer the world or at least our country. God made the world for us to live together in peace and not to fight.

Sincerely,
Samantha Smith

Perhaps no one person epitomized the underlying objective of the Goodwill Games better than young Samantha Smith, the original Goodwill Ambassador. With her childlike faith in the intrinsic unity of the human spirit, Samantha became an inspiration to even the world's most powerful leaders.

Shortly after her 1983 trip to the Soviet Union to meet Yuri Andropov, Samantha and her father died in a plane crash. Through the Samantha Smith Foundation, Jane Smith continues to work toward her daughter's goals. Together with Turner Broadcasting System, the Foundation organized "In the Spirit of Goodwill," an international youth art competition which attracted 10,000 entries from American and Soviet children. Two hundred of these drawings were exhibited during the Games as a tribute to Samantha and the Goodwill competition.

"Each generation contributes a building block for the next generation," stated Jane Smith. "As individuals, we are the particles of earth from which the blocks are formed. I hope Samantha has helped us realize how important each one of us can be. She stood fast in the belief that peace can be achieved and maintained by mankind."

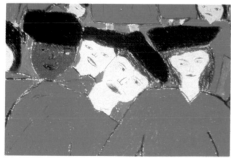

National Winner, Elementary School
"Graduation"
Vao Mataele
Royal Elementary School
Honolulu, Hawaii   11 Years Old

"In Hawaii, graduation from school is a happy time for friends and families. I can hardly wait until I graduate from school."

National Winner, Middle School
"Together In Goodwill"
Rusty Thrower
Bedford Junior High School
Hurst, Texas   14 Years Old

"I wanted to show ways we could forget our troubles and conflicts and come together in friendship during the Goodwill Games"

Amy Smith
Greenfield Junior High School
Greenfield, Ohio   14 Years Old

"I wanted to do something that no one else would try to do or even think of. A special message that everyone in the USSR and in the USA hoped for."

St. Basil's.

PEOPLE AND PLACES

American novelist Mark Twain once remarked, "The best way to learn about one's own-country is to visit another." In a page taken from the Goodwill Games' journal, Twain's words "hit home" for nearly 6,000 athletes, journalists and spectators who explored the 840 year-old city of Moscow as tourists.

Sportswriters by day became tourists at night. After filing their stories late in the evening, they left the world of athletics behind to walk beside the Kremlin in Red Square. There they witnessed the ceremonially stoic and symbolically sacred "changing of the guard" at Lenin's Tomb. Beneath the colorful spires of St. Basil's, which were enchanced by the glow of the midnight sun, the harsh sounds of the high-stepping guards' steel-heeled boots upon the cobblestones echoed across the empty square.

In the morning before the competition resumed, the guards' resounding hourly march was muffled by a sea of tourists and school children who filled the Square. In Gum department store, an expansive architectural wonder directly across from the Kremlin, shoppers swarmed in search of purchases ranging from socks to souvenirs. Others taxied off to the Bolshoi, imagining themselves as opening-night guests for the 19th Century premieres of "The Nutcracker Suite," "Swan Lake" or "Sleeping Beauty."

The day to return home arrived, and on that day nearly 6,000 people left Moscow. They departed leaving a part of themselves with the people they met. But remaining in the mind's eye — beyond the magnificence of St. Basil's and the beauty of the Bolshoi — was the warmth of the people from a distinctively different culture. The message in Mark Twain's travel advisory for those who made the journey to Moscow continues to make all the differences in the world dramatically more interesting, and potentially more rewarding.

Downtown Moscow at mid-day.

A Soviet veteran proudly displays his medals, ribbons and a Goodwill Games' button!

Gum Department Store.

A window in the Kremlin.

The "changing of the guard" at Lenin's Tomb.

The Kremlin and Lenin's Tomb in Red Square.

The Bolshoi

Galina Mezentseva and Vladimir Korolov of the Kirov Ballet.

CLOSING CEREMONY

Beneath a banner reading: "From Friendship In Sport To Peace On Earth" and a colorful display of flags representing 79 nations, a parade of trumpets sounded a festive chorus to announce the beginning of the Closing Ceremony.

The soothing performances of Kirov ballet dancers Galina Mezentseva and Vladimir Korolov were warmly applauded, and the accomplishments of Goodwill Games' athletes Jackie Joyner, Sergei Bubka, Debi Thomas and Galina Beloglazova were graciously honored in a ceremony celebrating a unity of culture of sport.

Those assembled in the Central Concert Hall saved their strongest ovation for the Games' founder, Ted Turner, who reflected upon the significance of the past 16 days of competition. Mr. Turner told the audience of 5,000, "These Games have proven that all the people in the world can cooperate in sports and other mutual endeavors – in a worthwhile and beneficial manner – irrespective of our differences." In a symbolic gesture characteristic of Mr. Turner's remarks, Marat Gramov, Chairman of the Soviet Committee on Physical Culture and Sport, presented a personal gift of peace to 1990 Host Committee Chairman, William Sullivan. The gift from Mr. Granov also came with a promise to Father Sullivan: to join him again – in the spirit of goodwill – when the athletes of the world reunite in four years' time on the playing fields of Seattle.

Ted Turner and Marat Gramlov congratulate Sergei Bubka for his world-record accomplishment.

Alexandr Vasilyev and Edwin Moses.

SEE YOU
IN SEATTLE

RESULTS

COUNTRY ABBREVIATIONS

AFG	Afghanistan	DOM	Dominican Republic	KUW	Kuwait	RWA	Rwanda
AHO	Netherlands Antilles	ECU	Ecuador	LAO	Laos	SAM	Western Samoa
ALB	Albania	EGY	Arab Rep. of Egypt	LBA	Libya	SAU	Saudi Arabia
ALG	Algeria	ESP	Spain	LBR	Liberia	SEN	Senegal
AND	Andorra	ETH	Ethiopia	LES	Lesotho	SEY	Seychelles
ANG	Angola	FIJ	Fiji (Islands)	LIB	Levanon	SIN	Singapore
ANT	Antigua	FIN	Finland	LIE	Liechtenstein	SLE	Sierra Leone
ARG	Argentina	FRA	France	LUX	Luxumborg	SMR	San Marino
AUS	Australia	FRG	Germany	MAD	Madagascar	ESA	El Salvador
AUT	Austria	GAB	Gabon	MAL	Malaysia	SOL	Solomon Islands
BAH	Bahamas	GAM	Gambia	MAR	Morocco	SOM	Somalia
BAN	Bangladesh	GBR	Great Britian	MAW	Malawi	SRI	Sri Lanka
BAR	Barbados	GDR	German Dem. Rep.	MDV	Maldives	SUD	Sudan
BEL	Belgium	GEQ	Equatorial Guinea	MEX	Mexico	SUI	Switzerland
BEN	Benin	GHA	Ghana	MGL	Mongolia	SUR	Surinam
BER	Bermuda	GRE	Greece	MLI	Mali	SWE	Sweden
BHU	Bhutan	GRN	Grenada	MLT	Malta	SWZ	Swaziland
BIR	Burma	GUA	Guatemala	MON	Monaco	SYR	Syria
BIZ	Belize	GUI	Guinea	MOZ	Mozambique	TAN	Tanzania
BOL	Bolivia	GUY	Guyana	MRI	Mauritius	TCH	Czechoslovikia
BOT	Botswana	HAI	Haiti	MTN	Mauritania	THA	Thailand
BRA	Brazil	HKG	Hong Kong	NCA	Nicaragua	TOG	Togo
BRN	Bahrain	HOL	Netherlands	NEP	Nepal	TGA	Tonga
BRU	Brunei	HON	Honduras	NGR	Nigeria	TPE	Chinese Taipei
BUL	Bulgaria	HUN	Hungary	NGU	Papua-New Guinea	TRI	Trinidad and Tobago
CAF	Central African Rep.	INA	Indonesia	NIG	Niger	TUN	Tunisia
CAN	Canada	IND	India	NOR	Norway	TUR	Turkey
CAY	Cayman Islands	IRL	Ireland	NZL	New Zealand	UAE	United Arab Emirates
CGO	Peoples Republic of Congo	IRN	Islamic Rep. of Iran	OMA	Oman	UGA	Uganda
CHA	Chad	IRQ	Iraq	PAK	Pakistan	URS	USSR
CHI	Chile	ISL	Iceland	PAN	Panama	USA	United States of America
CHN	People's Republic of China	ISR	Israel	PAR	Paraguay	VEN	Venezuela
CIV	Ivory Coast	ISV	Virgin Islands	PER	Peru	VIE	Vietnam
CMR	Cameroon	ITA	Italy	PHI	Phillippines	VOL	Burkinak-Faso
COL	Colombia	IVB	British Virgin Islands	POL	Poland	YAR	Yemen Arab Rep.
CRC	Costa Rica	JAM	Jamaica	POR	Portugal	YMD	Yemen Dem. Rep.
CUB	Cuba	JOR	Jordan	PRK	D.P.R. Korea	YUG	Yugoslavia
CYP	Cyprus	JPN	Japan	PUR	Puerto Rico	ZAI	Zaire
DEN	Denmark	KEN	Kenya	QAT	Qatar	ZAM	Zambia
DJI	Djibouti	KOR	Korea	ROM	Romania	ZIM	Zimbabwe

MEDAL TOTALS

Country	Gold	Silver	Bronze	Total	Country	Gold	Silver	Bronze	Total
URS	118	82	44	244	VEN	0	1	2	3
USA	42	47	51	140	POR	1	0	1	2
BUL	4	7	20	31	GBR	1	0	1	2
GDR	7	11	10	28	FRG	0	1	1	2
ROM	7	5	6	18	TUR	0	1	1	2
POL	2	3	6	11	BRA	0	0	2	1
TCH	0	8	2	10	ETH	1	0	0	1
CHN	0	4	5	9	SUI	1	0	0	1
PRK	1	0	5	6	NGR	0	1	0	1
HUN	0	1	5	6	PER	0	1	0	1
MGL	0	1	5	6	FIN	0	1	0	1
ITA	0	0	5	5	CIV	0	0	1	1
CAN	2	0	2	4	HOL	0	0	1	1
FRA	0	2	2	4	KEN	0	0	1	1
JPN	1	0	3	4	KUW	0	0	1	1
AUS	1	0	2	3	NOR	0	0	1	1

FINAL RESULTS

ATHLETICS – (Track & Field)

Women's 100m	Time
1. Evelyn Ashford (USA)	10.91
2. Heike Drechsler (GDR)	10.91
3. Elvira Barbashina (URS)	11.12
4. Alice Brown (USA)	11.14
5. Irina Slyusar (URS)	11.22
6. Antonina Nastoburko (URS)	11.29
7. Anelia Nuneva (BUL)	11.40
8. Angela Bailey (CAN)	11.50

Women's 200m	Time
1. Pam Marshall (USA)	22.12
2. Ewa Kasprzik (POL)	22.13
3. Elvira Barbashina (URS)	22.27
4. Gwen Torrence (USA)	22.53
5. Randy Givens USA)	22.61
6. Christine Cazier (FRA)	22.71
7. Juliet Cuthbert (JAM)	22.88
8. Maiya Azarashvili (URS)	23.01

Women's 400m	Time
1. Olga Vladykina (URS)	49.96
2. Maria Pinigina (URS)	50.29
3. Lillie Leatherwood (USA)	50.47
4. Diane Dixon (USA)	50.77
5. Genowefa Blaszak (POL)	51.52
6. Cristiana Matei (ROM)	51.57
7. Nadezhda Olizarenko (URS)	51.60
8. Olga Pesnopevtseva (URS)	51.86

Women's 800m	Time
1. Lyubov Gurina (URS)	1:57.52
2. Nadezhda Zabolotnov (URS)	1:57.54
3. Mitica Junghiatu (ROM)	1:57.87
4. Milena Strnadova (TCH)	1:57.90
5. Lyubov Kurnikova (URS)	1:58.69
6. Nadezhda Olizarenko (URS)	1:58.74
7. Claudette Groenendaal (USA)	1:59.31
8. Delisa Walton-Floyd (USA)	2:01.98

Women's 1500m	Time
1. Tatyana Samolenko (URS)	4:05.50
2. Ravilya Aglitdinova (URS)	4:06.14
3. Svetlana Kitova (URS)	4:07.21
4. Margareta Keszeg (ROM)	4:08.34
5. Mitica Jungiatu (ROM)	4:08.37
6. Nikolina Schereva (BUL)	4:10.71
7. Christine Gregorek (USA)	4:10.79
8. Linda Detlefsen (USA)	4:10.92

Women's 3000m	Time
1. Mariana Stanescu (ROM)	8:38.83
2. Svetlana Ulmasova (URS)	8:39.19
3. Regina Chistyakova (URS)	8:39.25
4. Elena Zhupiyeva (URS)	8:43.46
5. Patti Sue Plummer (USA)	8:46.24
6. Mary Knisely (USA)	8:49.00
7. Margareta Keszeg (ROM)	8:51.54
8. Cindy Bremser (USA)	8:53.74

Women's 5000m	Time
1. Olga Bondarenko (URS)	15:03.51
2. Svetlana Ulmasova (URS)	15:05.50
3. Cindy Bremser (USA)	15:11.78
4. Svetlana Guskova (URS)	15:17.90
5. Pattti Sue Plummer (USA)	15:20.88
6. Gabriello Woith (GDR)	15:21.90
7. Elena Zhupiyeva (URS)	15:23.55
8. Marina Rodchenkova (URS)	15:31.99

Women's Marathon	Time
1. Nadezhda Gumerova (URS)	2:33:09
2. Irina Bogacheva (URS)	2:34:09
3. Tatyana Gridneva (URS)	2:34:40
4. Irina Petrova (URS)	2:35:07
5. Yekaterina Khomenkova (URS)	2:35:47
6. Katy Schilly-Laetsch (USA)	2:36:22
7. Maureen Custy (USA)	2:36:44
8. Nadya Usmanova (URS)	2:37:43

Women's 10km Walk	Time
1. Kerry Saxby (AUS)	45:08.13
2. Ping Gun (CHN)	45:56.50

3. Aleksandra Grigorieva (URS)	46:00.27
4. Lidiya Levandovskaya (URS)	46:11.21
5. Vera Prudnikova (URS)	46:20.18
6. Elena Rodionova (URS)	46:41.08
7. Monika Gunnarsson (SWE)	47:02.65
8. Olga Krishtop (URS)	47:21.47

Women's 100m Hurdles	Time
1. Yordanka Donkova (BUL)	12.40
2. Cornelia Oschkenat (GDR)	12.62
3. Ginka Zagorchova (BUL)	12.72
4. Laurence Elloy (FRA)	12.75
5. Natalia Grigoryeva (URS)	12.86
6. Kerstin Knabe (GDR)	12.86
7. Vera Akimova (URS)	12.91
8. Elena Politika (URS)	12.97

Women's 400m Hurdles	Time
1. Marina Stepanova (URS)	53.81
2. Christiana Matei (ROM)	54.55
3. Ellen Fiedler (GDR)	54.80
4. Margarita Khromova (URS)	55.08
5. Elena Gorchkova (URS)	55.34
6. Judi Brown-King (USA)	56.06
7. Sandra Farmer (JAM)	56.28
8. Schowonda Williams (USA)	56.83

Women's 4 x 100m Relay	Time
1. USA (Michelle Finn, Diane Williams, Randy Givens, Evelyn Ashford)	42.12
2. URS (Olga Zolotareva, Maiya Azarashvili, Irina Slyusar, Elvira Barbashina)	42.27

Women's 4 x 400m Relay	Time
1. USA (Chandra Cheeseborough, Brenda Cliette, Lillie Leatherwood, Diane Dixon)	3:21.22
2. URS (Marina Stepanova, Maria Pinigina, Ludmila Dzhigalova, Olga Vladykina)	3:21.99

Women's High Jump	Feet/Meters
1. Stefka Kostadinova (BUL)	6'-8"/2.03
2. Olga Turchak (URS)	6'-7"/2.01
3. Svetla Isayeva (BUL)	6'-5"/1.96
Tamara Bykova (URS)	6'-5"/1.96
*5. Susanne Helm (GDR)	6'-5"/1.96
*6. Galina Brigadnaya (URS)	6'-5"/1.96
7. Andrea Binias (GDR)	6'-2¼"/1.89
Louise Ritter USA)	6'-2½"/1.89

Women's Long Jump	Feet/Meters
1. Galina Chistyakova (URS)	23'-20¾"/7.27
2. Elena Belevskaya (URS)	23'-6½"/7.17
3. Irina Valyukevich (URS)	23'-2½"/7.07
4. Vali Ionescu (ROM)	22'-8"/6.91
5. Carol Lewis (USA)	22'-7¾"/6.90
6. Helga Radtke (GDR)	22'-6¼"/6.86
7. Larisa Berezhnaya (URS)	22'-3¾"/6.69
8. Lyudmilla Ninova (URS)	21'-1½"/6.44

Women's Shot Put	Feet/Meters
1. Natalia Lisovskaya (URS)	70'-1½"/21.37
2. Natalia Akhrimenko (URS)	66'-8½"/20.33
3. Mihaela Loghin (ROM)	65'-3¼"/19.89
4. Marina Antonyuk (URS)	63'-4¾"/19.32
5. Svetlana Mitkova (BUL)	62'-8"/19.10
6. Danguole Bimbaite (URS)	62' 7¾"/19.00
7. Grit Haupt (GDR)	61'-8½"/18.81
8. Bonnie Dasse (USA)	60'-1¾"/18.33

Women's Discus	Feet/Meters
1. Tsvetanka Khristova (BUL)	228'-2"/69.54
2. Martina Hellmann (GDR)	226'-6"/69.04
3. Diana Sachse (GDR)	224'-7"/68.46
4. Ellina Zvereva (URS)	224'-2"/68.34
5. Lyubov Zverkova (URS)	211'-5"/64.44

6. Svetlana Mitkova (BUL)	206'-3"/62.88
7. Galina Yermakova (URS)	206'-3"/62.86
8. Larisa Korotkevich (URS)	196'-2"/59.88

Women's Javelin	Feet/Meters
1. Petra Felke (GDR)	232'-3"/70.78
2. Irina Kostyuchenkova (URS)	201'-0"/61.28
3. Natalia Yermolovich (URS)	198'-9"/60.56
4. Olga Gavrilova (URS)	195'-2"/59.48
5. Zinaida Gavrilina (URS)	190'-2"/57.96
6. Donna Mayhew (USA)	184'-4"/56.18
7. Karyn Szarkowski (USA)	165'-6"/50.44

Women's Heptathlon	Points
(NWR)*1. Jackie Joyner (USA)	7,148
2. Sybille Thiele (GDR)	6,635
3. Natalya Shubenkov (URS)	6,631
4. Sabine Paetz (GDR)	6,456
5. Marianna Maslennikova (URS)	6,416
6. Emilija Dimitrova (BUL)	6,403
7. Vaida Rushkite (URS)	6,349
8. Larisa Nikitina (URS)	6,285

Jackie Joyner's Record

	Time/Distance	Place	Points
1. 110 meter hurdles	12.85 sec.	1st	1,147
2. High Jump	6 ft. – 2 in.	1st(t)	1,080
3. Shot Put	48 ft. – 5¼ in.	4th	845
4. 200 meters	23.00 sec.	1st	1,079
5. Long Jump	23 ft. – 0 in.	1st	1,176
6. Javelin	163 ft. – 4 in.	2nd	857
7. 800 meters	2 min. 10.02 sec.	6th	964

Total: 7,148 Points

*(World Record – Old Record, 6,946, Sabine Paetz, GDR, 1984)

Men's 100m	Time
1. Ben Johnson (CAN)	9.95
2. Chidi Imoh (NGR)	10.04
3. Carl Lewis (USA)	10.06
4. Lee McRae (USA)	10.12
5. Vladimir Muraviev (URS)	10.20
6. Andrei Shlyapikov (URS)	10.21
Michael Morris (USA)	10.21
8. Harvey Glance (USA)	10.24

Men's 200m	Time
1. Floyd Heard (USA)	20.12
2. Dwayne Evans (USA)	20.45
3. Wallace Spearmon (USA)	20.49
4. Andrei Fedoriv (URS)	20.53
5. Vladimir Krylov (URS)	20.62
6. Nikolai Yushmanov (URS)	20.77
7. Nikolai Razgonov (URS)	20.83
8. David Lukuba (TAN)	22.19

Men's 400m	Time
1. Antonio McKay (USA)	44.98
2. Clarence Daniel (USA)	45.11
3. Darrell Robinson (USA)	45.15
4. Walter McCoy (USA)	45.56
5. Aleksandr Kurochkin (URS)	45.67
6. Danny Everett (USA)	45.94
7. Vladimir Posin (URS)	45.94
8. Vladimir Volodka (URS)	46.28

Men's 800m	Time
1. Johnny Gray (USA)	1:46.52
2. Stanley Redwine (USA)	1:46.89
3. Samuel Tirop (KEN)	1:47.05
4. Ryszard Ostrowski (POL)	1:47.25
5. Viktor Kalinkin (URS)	1:47.42
6. Nixon Kiprotich (KEN)	1:47.58
7. Vladimir Gradyn (URS)	1:47.80
8. Ahmed Belkessem (ALG)	1:47.86

Men's 1500m	Time
1. Pavel Yakovlev (URS)	3:39.96
2. Igor Lotorev (URS)	3:40.18
3. Steve Scott (USA)	3:40.31
4. Jim Spivey (USA)	3:40.41
5. Andreas Busse (GDR)	3:40.65
6. Jens-Peter Herold (GDR)	3:40.77
7. Sergei Afanasyev (URS)	3:40.97
8. Anatoli Legenda (URS)	3:41.17

Men's 3000m Steeplechase	Time
1. Hagen Melzer (GDR)	8:23.06
2. Henry Marsh (USA)	8:23.92
3. Nikolai Matyushenko (URS)	8:25.73
4. Micah Boinet (KEN)	8:28.20
5. Lev Glinskikh (URS)	8:29.51
6. Ivan Danu (URS)	8:30.74
7. Dzhozef Chelelgo (KEN)	8:33.03
8. Jim Cooper (USA)	8:33.77

Men's 5000m	Time
1. Doug Padilla (USA)	13:46.67
2. Terry Brahm (USA)	13:47.11
3. Evgueni Ignatov (BUL)	13:47.17
4. Mikhail Dasko (URS)	13:49.87
5. Axel Krippschok (GDR)	13:54.03
6. Vodadjo Bulti (ETH)	13:54.10
7. Spiros Andriopulos (GRE)	13:55.10
8. David Choge (KEN)	13:57.13

Men's 10,000m	Time
1. Domingos Castro (POR)	28:11.21
2. Gerard Donakowski (USA)	28:11.87
3. Dionisio Castro (POR)	28:12.04
4. Marcus Nenow (USA)	28:20.84
5. Takeyuki Nakayama (JPN)	28:23.63
6. Spiros Andriopulos (GRE)	28:27.23
7. Werner Schneider (GDR)	28:32.49
8. Shunichi Yoneshige (JPN)	28:37.32

Men's Marathon	Time
1. Belaine Dinsamo (ETH)	2:14:42
2. Igor Broslavsky (URS)	2:15:24
3. Yakov Tolstikov (URS)	2:16:22
4. Ravil Kashanov (URS)	2:17:10
5. Valentin Starikov (URS)	2:17:21
6. Sergei Rozum (URS)	2:17:54
7. Hi Bok Cho (PRK)	2:18:08
8. Alify Perevozchikov (URS)	2:18:51

Men's 20km Walk	Time
1. Aleksei Pershin (URS)	1:23.29
2. Aleksandr Boyarshinov (URS)	1:23.36
3. Yevgeny Misyulya (URS)	1:23.53
4. Guillaume Leblanc (CAN)	1:23.57
5. Anatoli Gorshkov (URS)	1:24.51
6. Vyacheslav Ivanenko (URS)	1:25.00
7. Yevgeny Yevsyukov (URS)	1:25.30
8. David Smith (AUS)	1:25.47

Men's 4 x 100m	Time
1. USA (Lee McRae, Floyd Heard, Harvey Glance, Carl Lewis)	37.98
2. URS (Aleksandr Yevgenyev, Nikolai Yushmanov, Vladimir Muravyev, Viktor Bryzgin)	38.19
3. URS (Aleksandr Kutepov, Roman Osipenko, Dmitri Bartenev, Sergei Klonov)	40.22
4. COL (Mauricio Domiguez, Juan Jose Viliamizar, Wilson Canizales, Arnui Cara Ursuriaga)	41.44

Men's 4 x 400m Relay	Time
1. URS (Vladimir Krylov, Vladimir Prosin, Vladimir Volodko, Aleksandr Kurochkin)	3:01.25
2. USA (Walter McCoy, Clarence Daniel, Danny Everett, Darrell Robinson)	3:01.47

Men's 110m Hurdles	Time
1. Greg Foster (USA)	13.25
2. Andrei Prokofyev (URS)	13.28
3. Keith Talley (USA)	13.31
4. Igor Perevedentsev (URS)	13.47
5. Aleksandr Markin (URS)	13.48
6. Igor Kazanov (URS)	13.50
Vladimir Shishkin (URS)	13.50
8. Don Wright (AUS)	13.65

Men's 400m Hurdles	Time
1. Edwin Moses (USA)	47.94
2. Aleksandr Vasilyev (URS)	48.24
3. David Patrick (USA)	48.59
4. Elhadji Amadou Ba (SEN)	48.73
5. Athanasious Kalogianis (GRE)	48.88
6. Toma Tomov (BUL)	49.08
7. Kevin Young (USA)	49.35
8. Oleg Azarov (URS)	49.38

Men's High Jump	Feet/Meters
1. Doug Nordquist (USA)	7'-8"/2.34
2. Igor Paklin (URS)	7'-7¼"/2.32
3. Sorin Matei (ROM)	7'-7¼"/2.32
4. Sergei Malchenko (URS)	7'-6"/2.29
5. Jan Zvara (TCH)	7'-6"/2.29
6. Rudolf Povarnitsyn (URS)	7'-4½"/2.25
7. Gennadi Avdeyenko (URS)	7'-4½"/2.25
8. Geoff Parsons (GBR)	7'-4½"/2.25

Men's Pole Vault	Feet/Meters
(NWR) *1. Sergei Bubka (URS)	19'-8¾"/6.01
2. Radion Gataullion(URS)	19'-0¼"/5.80
3. Earl Bell (USA)	18'-10¼"/5.75
4. Mike Tully (USA)	18'-8¼"/5.70
5. Aleksandr Krupski (URS)	18'-4½"/5.60
6. Vasily Bubka (URS)	18'-4½"/5.60
7. Frantisek Jansa (TCH)	17'-8½"/5.40
8. Phillipe Houvion (FRA)	17'-8½"/5.40

Men's Long Jump	Feet/Meters
1. Robert Emmiyan (URS)	28'-3"/8.61
2. Larry Myricks (USA)	27'-7¼"/8.41
3. Sergei Layevsky (URS)	26'-11"/8.20
4. Atanas Chochev (BUL)	25'-8¼"/7.83
5. Jan Laitner (TCH)	25'-8¼"/7.83
6. Klaus Beyer (GDR)	25'-8"/7.82
7. Atanas Atanasov (BUL)	25'-7¼"/7.80
8. Van Chi Tze (CHN)	25'-2½"/7.68

Men's Triple Jump	Feet/Meters
1. Mike Conley (USA)	56'-11½"/17.69
2. Khristo Markov (BUL)	56'-11¼"/17.35
3. Nikolai Musiyenko (URS)	56'-10¼"/17.33
4. Charlie Simpkins (USA)	56'-6½"/17.23
5. Aleksander Yakovlev (URS)	55'-9¼"/17.00
6. Poul Emordi (NGR)	54'-10¾"/16.73
7. Norifumi Yamashita (JPN)	54'-8¾"/16.68
8. Dirk Gamlin (GDR)	54'-6¼"/16.63

*(World Record – Old Record, 19'-8¼", Sergei Bubka, URS, Paris, 1985)

Men's Shot Put	Feet/Meters
1. Sergei Smirnov (URS)	71'-6"/21.79
2. Sergei Gavryushin (URS)	69'-2½"/21.09
3. John Brenner (USA)	67'-8"/20.62
4. Gregg Tafralis (USA)	66'-8"/20.32
5. Yanis Boyars (URS)	65'-11¾"/20.11
6. Dimitros Kutsukis (GRE)	62'-9¼"/19.13

Men's Dicus	Feet/Meters
1. Romas Ubartas (URS)	220'-2"/67.12
2. Dmitri Kovtsun (URS)	210'-9"/64.24
3. Knut Hjeltnes (NOR)	210'-0"/64.02
4. Imrich Bugar (TCH)	209'-4"/63.80
5. Georgi Kolnootchenko (URS)	207'-11"/63.38
6. Rick Meyer (USA)	205'-11"/62.76
7. Mike Buncic (USA)	201'-3"/61.34
8. Vasily Kaptyukh (URS)	196'-11"/60.02

Men's Hammer	Feet/Meters
1. Yuri Sedykh (URS)	227'-11"/84.72
2. Sergei Litvinov (URS)	277'-8"/84.64
3. Benyaminas Vituskis (URS)	262'-7"/80.04
4. Ralf Haber (GDR)	257'-6"/78.50
5. Igor Nikulin (URS)	257'-6"/78.50
6. Yuri Tamm (URS)	254'-3"/77.50
7. Jud Logan (USA)	245'-4"/74.78
8. Guenter Rodehau (GDR)	245'-1"/74.50

Men's Javelin	Feet/Meters
1. Tom Petranoff (USA)	273'-10"/83.46
2. Heino Puuste (URS)	272'-8"/83.12
3. Sergei Gavras (URS)	267'-2"/81.44
4. Viktor Yevsyukov (URS)	265'-2"/80.82
5. Einar Vilhjalmsson (ISL)	257'-11"/78.62
6. Marek Kaleta (URS)	256'-7"/78.22
7. Klaus-Jorg Murawa (GDR)	240'-7"/73.32
8. Bob Roggy (USA)	236'-1"/71.96

Men's Decathlon	Points
1. Gyorgi Degtyarov (URS)	8,322
2. Aleksandr Apaichev (URS)	8,244
3. Alaei Lyakh (URS)	8,082
4. Ens Peterson (GDR)	8,060
5. Ulrich Riecke (GDR)	8,000
6. Tim Bright (USA)	7,972
7. Uwe Freimuth (GDR)	7,950
8. Thomas Fahner (GDR)	7,939

WOMEN'S BASKETBALL

1. USA	(5-0)
2. URS	(4-1)
3. BRA	(3-2)
4. BUL	(2-3)
5. YUG	(1-4)
6. TCH	(0-5)

MEN'S WORLD BASKETBALL CHAMPIONSHIPS

Madrid, Spain

Team Competition
1. USA
2. URS
3. YUG
4. BRA
5. ESP
6. ITA
7. ISR
8. CAN
9. CHN
10. GRE
11. CUB
12. ARG

Championship Game:
USA 87
URS 85

Bronze Medal Game:
YUG 117
BRA 91

BOXING

Light Flyweight 48kg/106 pounds
1. Nshan Munchian (URS)
2. Karmizhan Abdrakhmanov (URS)
3. Enchkol Chan (PRK) and
   Tsenoidovyin Tserenniam (MGL)

Flyweight 51kg./112 pounds
1. Arthur Johnson (USA)
2. Rinvidas Bilus (URS)
3. David Griman (VEN) and
   Michael Vidinski (BUL)

Bantamweight 54kg./119 pounds
1. Alek Artemjev (URS)
2. Khvicha Khdrjan (URS)
3. Kim Chi Heri (PRK) and
   Bernard Price (USA)

Featherweight 57kg./125 pounds
1. Mikhak Kazarjan (URS)
2. Samson Khachatrain (URS)
3. Jose Luis Hernandez (VEN) and
   Frank Raushning (GDR)

Lightweight 60kg./132 pounds
1. Orzubek Nazarov (URS)
2. Romallis Ellis (USA)
3. Nerguiin Enhbat (MGL) and
   Juri Savochkin (URS)

Lightweight 63.5kg./139 pounds
1. Igor Ruzhnikov (URS)
2. Engels Pedroza (VEN)
3. Roy Jones (USA) and
   Erik Khakimov (URS)

Welterweight 67kg./147 pounds
1. Aleksandr Ostrovskij (URS)
2. Andrei Trocenko (URS)
3. Bogomil Aleksandrov (BUL) and
   Ricky Royal (USA)

Light Middleweight 71kg./156 pounds
1. Israel Akopkokhian (URS)
2. Viktor Egorov (URS)
3. Michael Moorer (USA) and
   Mylon Watkins (USA)

Middleweight 75kg./165 pounds
1. Ruslan Taramov (URS)
2. Parker White (USA)
3. Andrei Akulov (URS) and
   Lorenzo Wright (USA)

Light Heavyweight 81kg./178 pounds
1. Nurmagomed Shanavoz (URS)
2. Andrei Karavaev (URS)
3. Harvey Richards (USA) and
   Michael Simon (USA)

Heavyweight 91kg./201 pounds
1. Ramzan Sibiev (URS)
2. Vladimir Balay (URS)
3. Michael Bent (USA) and
   Ike Padilla (USA)

**Super Heavyweight
+91kg./+201 pounds**
1. Vyachislav Yakolev (URS)
2. Aleksandr Miroshnichenko (URS)
3. Ali Ahmed Baloushi (KUW) and
   Kilbert Pierce (USA)

CYCLING

Women's Sprints		Score
(NWR)	*1. Erika Salumiaee (URS)	(2-1)
	2 Galina Tsareva (URS)	
	3. Natalia Krusheinilskaya (URS)	(2-0)
	4. Zhou Siyin (CHN)	

Women's 3km Individual Pursuit	Time
1. Barbara Janz (SUI)	3:49.38
2. Melinda Mayfield (USA)	3:50.48
3. Galina Supron (URS)	3:52.34
4. Edith Schoenenberger (SUI)	3:56.78

Women's 20km Points Race	Points
1. Sally Hodge (GBR)	62
2. Tea Vikstadt-Nymna (FIN)	29
3. Galina Supron (URS)	20
4. Melinda Mayfield (USA)	16

Men's Sprints		Score
	1. Lutz Hesslich (GDR)	(2-0)
(NWR)	*2. Michael Hubner (GDR)	
	3. Gary Neiwand (AUS)	(2-0)
	4. Mark Gorski (USA)	

Men's 1km Time Trial	Time
1. Uldis Bremanis (URS)	1:03.566
2. Otar Mchedlishvili (URS)	1:04.583
3. Andreas Ganske (GDR)	1:05.422
4. Milan Hajek (TCH)	1:06.001

Men's 4km Individual Pursuit	Time
1. Vyacheslav Ekimov (URS)	4:26.07
2. Gintautas Umaras (URS)	4:30.75
3. Aleksandr Krasnov (URS)	4:30.91
4. Vasili Shpundov (URS)	4:32.40

Men's 4km Team Pursuit		Time
(NWR)	*1. URS (Vyacheslav Ekimov, Aleksandr Krasnov, Vasili Shpundov, Gintautas Umaras)	4:12.41
	2. TCH (Ales Trcka, Ctirad Fischer, Theodor Cerny, Pavel Soukup)	4:18.03
	3. AUS (Glenn Clarke, Brett Dutton, Wayne McCarthy, Dean Woods)	4:17.51

		Time
	4. POL (Rishard Davidovich, Roman Dvcharek, Andzhej Sikorski, Marian Turovski)	4:21.27

Men's Group Points	Points
1. Viktor Manakov (URS)	54
2. Ales Trcka (TCH)	38
3. Stancho Stanchev (BUL)	21
4. Miklos Somogyi (HUN)	16

*(Erika Salumiaee, URS. lowered the women's 200-meter flying start record to 11.489 breaking her own 1985 mark by .006 seconds)
*(Michael Hubner, GDR. lowered the men's 200-meter flying start mark to 10.244. The old mark of 10.249 was set by Sergei Kopylov, URS, in 1982)
*The Soviet team pursuit squad broke the world record twice, lowering the first mark to 4:12.83 in the qualifying round and then clocking 4:12.41 in the finals)

DIVING

Women's Springboard	Points
1. Brita Baldus (GDR)	493.02
2. Jianqin Li (CHN)	492.24
3. Zhanna Cirulnikova (URS)	476.64
4. Tristan Baker (USA)	476.07
5. Xiaoni Lin (CHN)	472.81
6. Katrin Bensing (GDR)	464.31
7. Michele Mitchell (USA)	461.40
8. Khandemarija Grecka (TCH)	452.22

Women's Platform	Points
1. Andezhela Stasjulevich (URS)	450.48
2. Olga Blinova (URS)	424.23
3. Michele Mitchell (USA)	414.63
4. Wendy Wyland (USA)	399.84
5. Xieqin Guan (CHN)	396.12
6. Hongxin Liu (CHN)	391.50
7. Khana Novotna (TCH)	368.31
8. Silke Abicht (GDR)	366.39

Men's Springboard	Points
1. Nikolai Drozhin (URS)	646.14
2. Kent Ferguson (USA)	643.32
3. Delyang Li (CHN)	622.86
4. Aleksei Kogalev (URS)	614.55
5. Doug Shaffer (USA)	600.81
6. Aleksandr Portnov (URS)	595.56
7. Rainer Punzel (GDR)	567.93
8. Ricardo Banuelos (MEX)	452.22

Men's Platform	Points
1. Sergei Gurylev (URS)	609.30
2. Dan Watson (USA)	593.34
3. Feng Gao (CHN)	569.55
4. Gennadi Starodubchev (URS)	566.46
5. Delyan Li (CHN)	559.20
6. Kent Ferguson (USA)	546.09
7. John Nash (CAN)	510.90
8. Craig Rogerson (AUS)	502.92

GYMNASTICS

Women's Team Competition

	Points
1. URS	196.10
2. BUL	190.60
3. CHN	190.25
4. ROM	189.25
5. USA	188.25
6. GDR	188.00
7. JPN	186.65

Women's All-Around Competition

	Points
1. Vera Kolesnikova (URS)	78.55
2. Elena Shushunova (URS)	78.40
3. Oksana Omelianchik (URS)	78.10
4. Gabriela Potorac (ROM)	77.00
5. Fang Luo (CHN)	76.70
6. Cuiting Shen (CHN)	76.60
7. Bojanka Demireva (BUL)	76.40
8. Mirela Sidion (ROM)	76.35

Women's Individual Events

Uneven Bars

	Points
1. Elena Shushunova (URS)	19.950
2. Vera Kolesnikova (URS)	19.650
3. Che Mil Huan (PRK)	19.550
4. Bojanka Demireva (BUL)	19.500
5. Gabriela Potorac (ROM)	19.425
6. Kim Gy Mok (PRK)	19.375
7. Chen Cuiting (CHN)	19.250
8. Ivelina Raikova (ROM)	18.950

Vault

	Points
1. Elena Shushunova (URS)	19.863
2. Elena Shevchenko (URS)	19.800
3. Joyce Wilborn (USA)	19.680
4. Gabriela Potorac (ROM)	19.550
5. Wang Hui Ying (CHN)	19.350
6. Mirela Sidion (ROM)	19.300
7. Angela Denkins (USA)	19.263
8. Chen Cuiting (CHN)	19.200

Balance Beam

	Points
1. Vera Kolesnikova (URS)	19.800
2. Elena Shushunova (URS)	19.725
3. Diana Dudeva (BUL)	19.400
4. Luo Fang (CHN)	19.250
5. Ivelina Raikova (BUL)	19.200
6. Chen Cuiting (CHN)	19.125
7. Jana Vogel (GDR)	19.075
8. Nerea Esbril Mil (ESP)	17.625

Floor Exercise

	Points
1. Elena Shushunova (URS)	19.875
2. Oksana Omelianchik (URS)	19.800
3. Mirela Sidion (ROM)	19.625
4. Joyce Wilborn (USA)	19.575
5. Hui Ying Wang (CHN)	19.500
6. Hope Spivey (USA)	19.475
7. Gabriela Potorac (ROM)	19.450
Diana Dudeva (BUL)	19.450

Men's Team Competition

	Points
1. URS	290.50
2. GDR	284.95
3. CHN	283.65
4. ROM	281.85
5. USA	281.20
6. JPN	280.30

Men's All-Around Competition

	Points
1. Yuri Korolev (URS)	117.15
2. Valentin Mogilny (URS)	116.55
3. Vladimir Artemov (URS)	116.45
4. Sylvio Kroll (GDR)	116.05
5. Chunsheng Wang (CHN)	115.15
6. Swen Tippelt (GDR)	114.45
7. Charles Lakes (USA)	114.10
8. Luming Fu (CHN)	113.90

Men's Individual Events

Floor Exercise

	Points
1. Yuri Korolev (URS)	19.70
2. Valentin Mogilny (URS)	19.65
Li Chungang (CHN)	19.65
4. Wang Chungseng (CHN)	19.55
5. Charles Lakes (USA)	19.35
6. Ulf Hoffmann (GDR)	19.30
7. Shigemitsu Kondo (JPN)	19.20
8. Yukihiro Hayase (JPN)	19.00

Pommel Horse

	Points
1. Valentin Mogilny (URS)	19.80
2. Yuri Korolev (URS)	19.70
3. Marian Risan (ROM)	19.50
4. Phil Cahoy (USA)	19.45
5. Sten Kepin-Fitsche (GDR)	19.40
6. Brian Babcock (USA)	19.15
7. Sylvio Kroll (GDR)	18.90
8. Shigemitsu Kondo (JPN)	18.40

Rings

	Points
1. Valentin Mogilny (URS)	19.65
Yuri Korolev (URS)	19.65
3. Sven Tippelt (GDR)	19.35
4. Marius Toba (ROM)	19.25
5. Kalofer Hristozov (BUL)	19.20
6. Ulf Hoffmann (GDR)	19.15
Fu Luming (CHN)	19.15
8. Valentin Pinter (ROM)	18.85

Vault

	Points
1. Valeri Lyukin (URS)	19.425
2. Marian Stoican (ROM)	19.300
3. (tie)Fan Ming (CHN)	19.275
Sylvio Kroll (GDR)	19.275
5. Yuri Korolev (URS)	19.200
6. Marius German (ROM)	19.100
7. Yukihiro Hayase (JPN)	19.075
8. Ulf Hoffmann (GDR)	18.925

Parallel Bars

	Points
1. Valentin Mogilny (URS)	19.65
Le Chen Hol (PRK)	19.65
3. Sven Tippelt (GDR)	19.55
4. Holger Berendt (GDR)	19.45
5. Marius German (ROM)	19.30
Phil Cahoy (USA)	19.30
7. Aleksandr Tikhonkikh (URS)	19.20
8. Marian Rizan (ROM)	18.60

High Bar

	Points
1. Yuri Korolev (URS)	19.80
2. Chunsheng Wang (CHN)	19.65
Zsolt Borkai (HUN)	19.65
4. Linsheng Go (CHN)	19.60
5. Sylvio Kroll (GDR)	19.50
6. Chol Nam Kim (PRK)	19.40
7. Vladimir Artemov (URS)	19.15
8. Maarius German (ROM)	19.00

All-Around Competition

	Points
1. Tatyana Druchinina (URS)	40.00
2. Marina Lobach (URS)	39.90
3. Galina Beloglazova (URS)	39.85
4. Svetomira Filipova (BUL)	39.50
5. Florentina Butaru (ROM)	39.35
6. Adriana Dunavska (BUL)	39.30
7. Albena Naidova (BUL)	39.15
Bianka Dittrich (GDR)	39.15

Rope Competition

	Points
1. Bianka Dittrich (GDR)	20.00
Marina Lobach (URS)	20.00
Tatyana Druchinina (URS)	20.00
4. En Lan Kan (PRK)	19.90
Svetomira Filipova (BUL)	19.90
6. Florentina Butaru (ROM)	19.80
7. Albena Naidova (BUL)	19.70
8. Eeva-Liisa Narhi (FIN)	19.50

Ball Competition

	Points
1. Galina Beloglazova (URS)	20.00
Tatyana Druchinina (URS)	20.00
3. Svetomira Filipova (BUL)	19.80
4. Florentina Butaru (ROM)	19.70
Albena Naidova (BUL)	19.70
6. Ok Sun Tian (PRK)	19.65
7. Esther Niklas (GDR)	19.50
8. Moncerrat Manzanares (ESP)	19.45

TEAM HANDBALL

Women's Team Competition

1. URS	(5-0)
2. FRG	(4-1)
3. HUN	(3-2)
4. DEN	(2-3)
5. JPN	(1-4)
6. USA	(0-5)

Men's Team Competition

1. URS	(4-0)
2. USA	(2-2)
3. TCH	(2-2)
4. ISL	(1-3)
5. POL	(1-3)

JUDO

EXTRA LIGHTWEIGHTS: 60kg./138 lbs.
1. Mikihiro Mukai (JPN)
2. Igor Zhuckov (URS)
3. Kak Jon (PRK)
   Raffaele Rennella (ITA)

HALF LIGHTWEIGHTS: 65kg/143 lbs.
1. Ali Khamkhoyev (URS)
2. Igor Glyuuk (URS)
3. Tamas Bujko (HUN)
   Motohiro Koga (JPN)

LIGHTWEIGHTS: 71kg./156 lbs.
1. Igor Shkarin (URS)
2. Yuri Sokolov (URS)
3. Veslav Blakh (POL)
   Kenneth Brown (GBR)

HALF MIDDLEWEIGHTS: 78kg./172 lbs.
1. Vladimir Shestakov (URS)
2. Marcel Pietri (FRA)
3. Giorgi Vismara (ITA)
   Ganbold Zhambalyn (MGL)

MIDDLEWEIGHTS: 86kg./189 lbs.
1. Aleksandr Sivtsev (URS)
2. Vitaly Pesynak (URS)
3. Francois Fournier (FRA)
   Roland Borawski (GDR)

HALF HEAVYWEIGHTS: 95kg./209 lbs.
1. Viktor Poddubryi (URS)
2. Baldzhinniam Odvoin (MGL)
3. Gilles Jaladon (FRA)
   Irji Sosna (TCH)

HEAVYWEIGHTS: +95kg./+209 lbs.
1. Grigori Verichev (URS)
2. Steve Cohen (USA)
3. Andzhej Basik (POL)
   Che Hgil Khuan (PRK)

NO WEIGHT LIMIT: Open Category
1. Khabil Biktashev (URS)
2. Anzhej Basik (POL)
3. Dimitr Zapryanov (BUL)
   Ryuri Okada (JPN)

MODERN PENTATHLON

Women's Team Competition

	Points
1. POL	15,183
2. URS	14,913
3. FRG	14,882
4. FRA	14,816
5. USA	14,517
6. HUN	14,501
7. ITA	13,808
8. GBR	13,547

Women's Individual Competition

	Points
1. Tatyana Chernetskaya (URS)	5,280
2. Sophie Moressee (FRA)	5,232
3. Lori Norwood (USA)	5,175
4. Barbara Kotowksa (POL)	5,133
5. Pernille Neilsen (DEN)	5,120
6. Caroline Delemer (FRA)	5,082
7. Andrea Tuck (HUN)	5,068
8. Katrin Kroning (FRG)	5,066

Men's Team Competition

	Points
1. URS	16,607
2. POL	15,557
3. HUN	15,294
4. USA	15,106
5. TCH	15,099
6. ITA	15,075
7. BUL	14,803
8. ESP	14,306

Men's Individual Competition

	Points
1. Vakhtang Yagorashvilll (URS)	5,581
2. Anatoli Avdeyev (URS)	5,522
3. Igor Schvartz (URS)	5,495
4. Herman Yuferov (URS)	5,479
5. Anatoly Starostin (URS)	5,466
6. Yevgeni Lipeyev (URS)	5,385
7. Sergei Gosudarev (URS)	5,339
8. Aleksandr Poddubny (URS)	5,323

MOTOBALL

Game 1 (Exhibition)
URS – 5
Europe – 2

Game 2 (Exhibition)
URS – 7
Europe – 3

ROWING

Women's Single Sculls	Time
1. Antonia Dumcheva (URS)	7:33.33
2. Anne Marden (USA)	7:55.95

Women's Lightweight
Single Sculls	Time
1. Angie Herron (USA)	7:53.05
2. Tatyana Mironova (URS)	7:59.15

Women's Pairs
Without Coxswain	Time
1. URS (Marina Pegova, Galina Stepanova)	7:25.76
2. USA (Pamela Knapp, Jennifer Scott)	7:36.26

Women's Fours
With Coxswain	Time
1. URS (Sarmite Stone, Inga Kryuchkina, Laima Daneikaite, Nadezhda Sugako, Galina Ruda)	6:52.47
2. USA (Margaret Mallery, Alison Townley, Mara Keggi, Abby Peck, Kim Santiago)	6:54.47

Women's Fours
Without Coxswain	Time
1. URS (Irina Klyshevskaya, Stella Melnichuk, Marina Zhukova, Svetlana Mazii)	6:25.60
2. USA (Ann Strayer, Jennie Marshall, Beth Holasak, Evelyn Harmann)	6:32.49

Women's Eights	Time
1. URS (Marina Suprun, Sariya Zakirova, Elena Pukhayeva, Marina Znak, Irina Teterina, Lidya Averyanova, Vida Tsesyunaite, Elena Tereshina, Valentina Khokhlova)	
2. USA (Sara Nevin, Pamela Knapp, Jennifer Scott, Nancy Barnett, Alison Townley, Margaret Mallery, Abby Peck, Mara Keggi, Kim Santiago)	6:33.67

Men's Single Sculls	Time
1. Vasili Yakusha (URS)	7:05.63
2. Greg Springer (USA)	7:15.68

Men's Lightweight
Single Sculls	Time
1. Vladimir Mityushev (URS)	7:19.30
2. Brian Benz (USA)	7:28.38

Men's Pairs
Without Coxswain	Time
1. URS (Yuri Pimenov, Nikolai Pimenov)	6:35.07
2. USA (Michael Tati, John Strotback)	6:37.31

Men's Fours
With Coxswain	Time
1. URS (Ivan Vystosky, Sigitas Kuchinskas, Vladimir Romanishin, Igor Zotov, Mikhail Sasov)	6:04.83
2. USA (William Burden, Jonathan Smith, Kurt Bausback, Chris Huntington, Mark Zembsch)	6:07.45

Men's Eights	Time
1. USA (Jonathan Kissick, Chris Penny, John Terwilliger, Dave Kmpotich, Tom Kiefer, Edward Ives, Kevin Still, Andy Sudduth, Jonathan Fish)	5:36.98
2. URS (Nikolai Komarov, Veniamin But, Viktor Omelijanovich, Jonas Narmontas, Viktor Diduk, Pavel Gurkovskij, Gennadi Krujchkin, Jonas Pinskus, Gyorgi Dmitrenko)	5:41.22

SWIMMING

Women's 50m Freestyle	Time
1. Angel Myers (USA)	25.60
2. Inna Abramova (URS)	26.18
Kathy Coffin (USA)	26.18
4. Kerstin Kielgas (GDR)	26.89
5. Irina Gapon (URS)	26.94
6. Peggi Ehnikhen (GDR)	28.16

Women's 100m Freestyle	Time
1. Angel Myers (USA)	56.48
2. Kathy Coffin (USA)	56.93
3. Paige Zemina (USA)	56.97
4. Kerstin Kielgas (GDR)	57.84
5. Dagmar Hase (GDR)	57.96
6. Elena Dendeberova (URS)	58.20
7. Inna Abramova (URS)	58.48
8. Stacy Cassidy (USA)	58.64

Women's 200m Freestyle	Time
1. Kerstin Kielgas (GDR)	2.01.91
2. Dagmar Hase (GDR)	2:02.99
3. Stacy Cassidy (USA)	2:03.15
4. Lisa Gillespie (USA)	2:03.76
5. Elena Dendeberova (URS)	2:04.09
6. Julia Gorman (USA)	2:04.29
7. Svetlana Kopchikova (URS)	2:04.42
8. Anke Moering (GDR)	2:05.59

Women's 400m Freestyle	Time
1. Kathy Hettche (USA)	4:11.53
2. Anke Moering (GDR)	4:12.50
3. Noemi Lung (ROM)	4:12.53
4. Leslie Daland (USA)	4:13.89
5. Janet Evans (USA)	4:16.74
6. Andrea Orosz (HUN)	4:17.91
7. Grit Richter (GDR)	4:19.01
8. Eniko Palencsar (SYR)	4:20.51

Women's 800m Freestyle	Time
1. Leslie Daland (USA)	8:30.40
2. Kathy Hettche (USA)	8:30.80
3. Janet Evans (USA)	8:38.07
4. Anke Moering (GDR)	8:39.09
5. Grit Rikhter (GDR)	8:44.37
6. Enika Palencsar (ROM)	8:45.26
7. Jennifer Linder (USA)	8:45.64
8. Antonaneta Strumenlieva (BUL)	8:57.38

Women's 1500m Freestyle	Time
1. Leslie Daland (USA)	16:15.88
2. Anke Moering (GDR)	16:20.30
3. Janet Evans (USA)	16:24.92
4. Enika Palenscar (ROM)	16:34.95
5. Jennifer Linder (USA)	16:38.46
6. Grit Richter (GDR)	16:47.12
7. Antonaneta Strumenlieva (BUL)	17:02.03
8. Natalia Kuzmina (URS)	17:04.96

Women's 100m Backstroke	Time
1. Carmen Bunaciu (ROM)	1:02.63
2. Aneta Patrasciou (ROM)	1:02.63
3. Natalia Shibaeva (URS)	1:02.93
4. Birte Weigang (GDR)	1:03.30
5. Laura McLean (USA)	1:03.43
6. Marion Sperka (GDR)	1:03.74
7. Beth Barr (USA)	1:03.88
9. Tori Trees (USA)	1:04.38

Women's 200m Backstroke	Time
1. Aneta Patrasciou (ROM)	2:11.69
2. Andrea Hayes (USA)	2:13.99
3. Laura McLean (USA)	2:14.62
4. Natalia Shibayeva (URS)	2:15.02
5. Beth Barr (USA)	2:15.45
6. Marion Sperka (GDR)	2:16.49
7. Tori Trees (USA)	2:18.78
8. Irina Tolstaya (URS)	2:20.58

Women's 100m Breaststroke	Time
1. Tanya Bogomilova (BUL)	1:10.21
2. Elena Volkova (URS)	1:10.46
3. Kathy Smith (USA)	1:12.26
4. Natalia Kuzmina (URS)	1:12.64
5. Peggi Ehnikhen (GDR)	1:13.03
6. Larisa Moreva (URS)	1:13.13
7. Dorota Chulak (POL)	1:13.80
8. Amy Shaw (USA)	1:13.96

Women's 200m Breaststroke	Time
1. Elena Volkova (URS)	2:29.84
2. Tanya Bogomilova (BUL)	2:30.93
3. Amy Shaw (USA)	2:33.43
4. Larisa Moreva (URS)	2:33.98
5. Suzana Bernike (GDR)	2:34.39
6. Kathy Smith (USA)	2:35.80
7. Natalia Miroshnik (URS)	2:36.01
8. Peggi Ehnikhen (GDR)	2:36.31

Women's 100m Butterfly	Time
1. Birte Weigang (GDR)	1:00.36
2. Carmen Bunaciu (ROM)	1:01.56
3. Angel Myers (USA)	1:01.74
4. Kelley Davies (USA)	1:01.93
5. Melanie Buddemeyer (USA)	1:01.94
6. Tatyana Kurnikova (URS)	1:02.16
7. Terri O'Laughlin (USA)	1:02.58
8. Bistra Gospodinova (BUL)	1:03.27

Women's 200m Butterfly	Time
1. Kelley Davies (USA)	2:12.49
2. Julia Gorman (USA)	2:13.60
3. Jennifer Linder (USA)	2:14.29
4. Elena Osadchuk (URS)	2:15.34
5. Tatyana Kurnikova (URS)	2:17.62
6. Inna Bajermann (FRG)	2:24.53

Women's 200m
Individual Medley	Time
1. Noemi Lung (ROM)	2:17.32
2. Elena Dendeberova (URS)	2:18.03
3. Tanya Bogomilov (BUL)	2:18.68
4. Sonia Blagova (BUL)	2:18.87
5. Andrea Hayes (USA)	2:18.91
6. Julia Gorman (USA)	2:19.09
7. Svetlana Kopchikova (URS)	2:19.95
8. Suzana Bernike (GDR)	2:21.20

Women's 400m

Individual Medley	Time
1. Noemi Lung (ROM)	4:43.17
2. Andrea Hayes (USA)	4:51.47
3. Sonia Blagova (BUL)	4:52.40
4. Elena Dendeberova (URS)	4:52.86
5. Svetlana Kopchikova (URS)	4:56.29
6. Janet Evans (USA)	4:59.80

Women's 4 x 100m

Individual Medley Relay	Time
1. USA (Laura McLean, Kathy Smith, Kelley Davies, Angel Myers)	4:12.54
2. URS (Natalia Shibaeva, Elena Volkova, Tatyana Kurnikova, Elena Dendeberova)	4:13.15 (NWR)
3. USA (Beth Barr, Amy Shaw, Melanie Buddemeyer, Kathy Coffin)	4:15.33
4. USA (Tori Trees, Christy Richardson, Terri O'Laughlin, Paige Zemina)	4:16.64
5. BUL (Sonia Blagova, Tanya Bogomilova, Bistra Gospodinova, Vania Argirova)	4:18.02
6. URS (Irina Tolstaja, Natalina Kuzmina, Elena Osadchik, Svetlana Kopchikova)	4:06.03

Women's 4 x 100m

Freestyle Relay	Time
1. USA (Kathy Coffin, Paige Zemina, Angel Myers, Stacy Cassidy)	3:47.68
2. URS (Svetlana Kopchikova, Inna Abramova, Tatyana Kurnikova, Elena Dendeberova)	3:51.21
3. USA (Melanie Buddemeyer, Julie Gorman, Lisa Gillespie, Kelley Davies)	3:52.19
4. URS (Kerstin Kielgas, Dagmar Hase, Anke Moering, Grit Rikhter)	3:53.39

Women's 4 x 200m

Freestyle Relay	Time
1. USA (Paige Zemina, Julie Gorman, Kathy Coffin, Andrea Hayes)	8:10.49
2. USA (Kathy Hettche, Lisa Gillespie, Kelley Davies, Stacy Cassidy)	8:11.08
3. GDR (Dagmar Hase, Grit Rikhter, Anke Moering, Kerstin Kielgas)	8:11.58
4. BUL (Vania Argirova, Antonaneta Strumenlieva, Tania Bogomilova, Sonia Blagova)	8:34.37
5. URS (Svetlana Kopchikova, Anna Rezer, Elena Osadchuk, (Natalia Kuzmina)	8:46.04

Men's 50m Freestyle

	Time
1. John Sauerland (USA)	23.13
2. Gennadi Prigoda (URS)	23.34
3. Sergei Smiryagin (URS)	23.37
4. Monut Musat (ROM)	23.48
5. Nikolai Yevseyev (URS)	23.49
6. Adam Schmitt (USA)	23.58
7. Dave Kerska (USA)	23.89
8. Randy Everatt (USA)	24.54

Men's 100m Freestyle

	Time
1. Nikolai Yevseyev (URS)	50.47
2. Sergei Smiryagin (URS)	50.97
3. Dave Kerska (USA)	51.09
4. Gennadi Prigoda (URS)	51.17
5. John Sauerland (USA)	51.61
6. Randy Everatt (USA)	51.68
7. Venyamin Tayanovich (URS)	51.76
8. Adam Schmidt (USA)	52.54

Men's 200m Freestyle

	Time
1. John Witchell (USA)	1:50.17
2. Nikolai Yevseyev (URS)	1:50.32
3. Paul Robinson (USA)	1:51.00
4. Aleksandr Chayev (URS)	1:51.62
5. Steffen Lless (GDR)	1:52.13
6. Venyamin Tayanovich (URS)	1:52.36
7. Sean Killion (USA)	1:52.41
8. Jeff Prior (USA)	1:52.94

Men's 400m Freestyle

	Time
1. Sean Killion (USA)	3:51.91
2. Vladimir Salnikov (URS)	3:52.00
3. Scott Brackett (USA)	3:52.31
4. Jeff Prior (USA)	3:53.81
5. Steffen Leiss (GDR)	3:54.80
6. John Witchell (USA)	3:55.31
7. Eduard Petrov (URS)	3:55.82
8. Akhmad Hussein (SYR)	4:16.44

Men's 800m Freestyle

	Time
1. Vladimir Salnikov (URS)	*7:50.64
2. Eduard Petrov (URS)	8:00.96
3. Sean Killion (USA)	8:02.09
4. Scott Brackett (USA)	8:02.96
5. Steffen Liess (GDR)	8:07.34
6. Jeff Erwin (USA)	8:09.12
7. Aleksandr Gaydukevich (URS)	8:21.01
8. Carlos Scanavino (URU)	8:33.26

Men's 150m Freestyle

	Time
1. Vladimir Slanikov (URS)	15:10.87
2. Scott Brackett (USA)	15:17.34
3. Eduard Petov (URS)	15:25.28
4. Jeff Erwin (USA)	15:31.70
5. Steffen Lless (GDR)	15:37.32
6. Tamas Daryni (HUN)	15:44.84
7. Ahmed Hussein (SYR)	16:52.59

Men's 100m Backstroke

	Time
1. Igor Polyansky (URS)	56.02
2. Sergei Zabolotnov (URS)	56.13
3. Oleg Gavrilenko (URS)	56.86
4. Andy Gill (USA)	57.13
5. Charles Siroky (USA)	57.50
6. Chris O'Neil (USA)	1:01.80
7. Eric Greenwood (CRC)	1:04.52

Men's 200m Backstroke

	Time
1. Igor Polyansky (URS)	1:58.73
2. Sergei Zabolotov (URS)	2:00.10
3. Oleg Gavrilenko (URS)	2:02.50
4. Charles Siroky (USA)	2:04.84
5. Zoltan Balajti (HUN)	2:06.04
6. Andy Gill (USA)	2:06.64
7. Karsten Schultz (GDR)	2:09.81
8. Eric Greenwood (CRC)	2:18.30

Men's 100m Breaststroke

	Time
1. Dmitri Volkov (URS)	1:03.69
2. Eduard Klimentev (URS)	1:04.29
3. Timur Podmarev (URS)	1:04.49
4. Mark Vondermey (USA)	1:04.84
5. Valeri Lozik (URS)	1:05.11
6. George Koch (USA)	1:05.16
7. Ingo Grizivotz (GDR)	1:07.25

Men's 200m Breaststroke

	Time
1. Dimitri Volkov (URS)	2:17.72
2. Valeri Lozik (URS)	2:18.42
3. Timur Podmarev (URS)	2:18.44
4. Eduard Klimentev (URS)	2:19.25
5. Mark Vandermey (USA)	2:20.04
6. Peter Szabo (HUN)	2:20.41
7. George Koch (USA)	2:21.65
8. Ingo Grzivuto (GDR)	2:24.02

Men's 100m Butterfly

	Time
1. Chris O'Neil (USA)	54.23
2. Ken Flaherty (USA)	54.88
3. Sergei Garro (URS)	55.11
4. Konstantin Petrov (URS)	55.16
5. Markel Geru (TCH)	55.26
6. Aleksei Markovsky (URS)	55.31
7. Melvin Stewart (USA)	56.06
8. Stefan Gusgen (FRG)	56.19

Men's 200m Butterfly

	Time
1. Melvin Stewart (USA)	2:00.83
2. Matt Rankin (USA)	2:00.91
3. Ken Flaherty (USA)	2:01.06
4. Bill Stapleton (USA)	2:02.16
5. Dmitri Pankov (URS)	2:02.35
6. Aleksandr Prigoda (URS)	2:02.80
7. Konstantin Petrov (URS)	2:03.13
8. Marek Izydorchik (POL)	2:04.17

Men's 200m Individual Medley

	Time
1. Vadim Yaroshchuk (URS)	2:02.83
2. Billy Stapleton (USA)	2:03.36
3. Ron Karnaugh (USA)	2:04.56
4. Aleksandr Sidorenko (URS)	2:05.66
5. Matt Rankin (USA)	2:05.67
6. Jeff Prior (USA)	2:05.78
7. Sergei Pichugin (URS)	2:06.47
8. Christian Gessner (GDR)	2:07.08

Men's 400m

Individual Relay	Time
1. Vadim Yaroshchuk (URS)	4:22.06
2. Billy Stapleton (USA)	4:23.42
3. Matt Rankin (USA)	4:25.02
4. Jeff Prior (USA)	4:26.23
5. Sergei Marinyuk (URS)	4:28.25
6. Kristian Gessner (GDR)	4:29.39
7. Sergei Pichugin (URS)	4:30.12
8. Holger Aekhoff (FRG)	4:40.77

Men's 4 x 100m

Individual Medley Relay	Time
1. URS (Igor Polyansky, Dmitri Volkov, Sergei Garro, Nikolai Yevseyev)	3:42.83
2. URS (Sergei Zabolotnov, Eduard Klimentev, Aleksei Markovsky, Sergei Smiryagin)	3:43.66
3. USA (Charles Siroky, George Koch, Ken Flaherty, Dave Kerska)	3:46.03
4. URS (Oleg Gavrilenko, Timur Podmarev, Konstantin Petrov, Aleksandr Prigoda)	3:46.31
5. FRG (Michael Grebe, Holger Aekhoff, Andreas Berend, Steffan Gusten)	4:00.02

Men's 4 x 100m

Freestyle Relay	Time
1. URS (Sergei Smiryagin, Gennadi Prigoda, Aleksei Markovsky, Nikolai Yevseyev)	3:20.77
2. USA (Randy Everatt, Dave Kerska, Paul Robinson, John Sauerland)	3:23.52
3. USA (Adam Schmitt, Charley Siroky, Ron Karnaugh, Chris O'Neil)	3:29.36
4. FRG (Andreas Berend, Holdger Aikhoff, Michael Artinger, Stefan Gusgen)	3:34.74

Men's 4 x 400m

Freestyle Relay	Time
1. USA (Paul Robinson, Sean Killion, Randy Everatt, John Wichell)	7:21.75
2. URS (Veniamin Tayanovich, Gennadi Prigoda, Aleksandr Chaev, Nikolai Yevseyev)	7:21.83
3. USA (Jeff Prior, Charley Siroky, Dave Kerska, Scott Brackett)	7:26.84

TENNIS

Women's Singles

1. Caroline Kuhlman (USA)
2. Beverly Bowes (USA)
3. Svetlana Parkhomenko (URS)
4. Larisa Savchenko (URS)

Women's Doubles

1. Svetlana Parkhomenko and Larisa Savchenko (URS)
2. Iva Budarova and Marcella Skuherska (TCH)
3. Caroline Kuhlman and Ronni Reis (USA)
4. Leila Meskhi and Natalia Zvereva (URS)

Men's Singles

1. Andrei Chesnokov (URS)
2. Marian Vajda (TCH)
3. Brad Pearce (USA)
4. Aleksandr Zverev (URS)

Men's Doubles
1. Sergei Leonyuk and
   Aleksandr Zverev (URS)
2. Marian Vajda and
   Karel Novacek (TCH)
3. Luke Jensen and
   Brad Pearce (USA)
4. Jay Berger and
   Kelly Jones (USA)

VOLLEYBALL

Women's Team Competition
1. URS	(5-0)
2. PER	(3-2)
3. USA	(2-3)
4. JPN	(2-3)
5. PRK	(2-3)
6. TCH	(1-4)
7. GDR	(1-4)
8. FRG	(0-5)

Men's Team Competition
1. URS	(5-0)
2. USA	(4-1)
3. JPN	(2-3)
4. FRA	(3-2)
5. BUL	(3-2)
6. TCH	(2-3)
7. POL	(1-4)
8. BRA	(1-4)

WATER POLO

Men's Team Competition
1. URS	(5-0-0)
2. USA	(3-1-1)
3. HUN	(2-1-2)
4. FRG	(2-2-1)
5. HOL	(1-4-0)
6. GRE	(0-5-0)

WEIGHTLIFTING

100 kg./220 lbs.

Overall
	Total
1. Ruslan Balaev (URS)	412.5 kg./909.25 lbs.
2. Nicu Vlad (ROM)	410.0 kg./903.75 lbs.
3. Yus Dandik (URS)	405.0 kg./892.75 lbs.
4. Detelin Petrov (BUL)	400.0 kg./881.75 lbs.
5. Piotr Krukowski (POL)	395.0 kg./870.75 lbs.
6. Stefan Khristov (BOL)	380.0 kg./837.50 lbs.
7. Janos Bofki (HUN)	365.0 kg./804.50 lbs.
8. Mathias Muller (GDR)	350.0 kg./771.50 lbs.

Snatch
	Total
1. Nicu Vlad (ROM)	187.5 kg./413.25 lbs.
2. Yuri Dandik (URS)	187.5 kg./413.25 lbs.
3. Ruslan Balaev (URS)	185.0 kg./407.50 lbs.
4. Detelin Petrov (BUL)	180.0 kg./396.75 lbs.
5. Piotr Krukowski (POL)	175.0 kg./385.75 lbs.
6. Zoltan Balazsfi (HUN)	165.0 kg./363.75 lbs.
7. Janos Bokfi (HUN)	165.0 kg./363.75 lbs.
8. Stefan Khristov (BUL)	160.0 kg./352.50 lbs.

Clean and Jerk
	Total
1. Ruslan Balaev (URS)	227.5 kg./501.50 lbs.
2. Nicu Vladm (ROM)	222.5 kg./490.50 lbs.
3. Piotr Krukowski (POL)	220.0 kg./485.00 lbs.
4. Detelin Petrov (BUL)	220.0 kg./485.00 lbs.
5. Stefan Khristov (BUL)	220.0 kg./485.00 lbs.
6. Yuri Dandik (URS)	217.5 kg./479.50 lbs.
7. Janos Bokfi (HUN)	200.0 kg./440.75 lbs.
8. Mathias Muller (GDR)	197.5 kg./435.25 lbs.

110 kg./242.50 lbs.

Overall
	Total
1. Yuri Zakharevich (URS)	417.5 kg./920.25 lbs.
2. Anton Baraniak (TCH)	407.5 kg./898.25 lbs.
3. Norberto Oberburger (ITA)	392.5 kg./865.25 lbs.
4. Jozef Jacso (HUN)	370.0 kg./815.50 lbs.
5. Istvan Sandor (HUN)	365.0 kg./804.50 lbs.
6. Stanislav Malysa (POL)	362.5 kg./799.00 lbs.
7. Frank Hartmann (GDR)	342.5 kg./755.00 lbs.
8. Ken Clark (USA)	332.5 kg./733.00 lbs.

Snatch
	Total
1. Yuri Zakharevich (URS)	187.5 kg./413.25 lbs.
2. Anton Baraniak (TCH)	182.5 kg./402.25 lbs.
3. Norberto Oberburger (ITA)	177.5 kg./391.25 lbs.
4. Jozef Jacso (HUN)	170.0 kg./374.75 lbs.
5. Stanislav Malysa (POL)	165.0 kg./363.75 lbs.
6. Istvan Sandor (HUN)	160.0 kg./352.50 lbs.
7. Frank Hartmann (GDR)	152.5 kg./336.00 lbs.
8. Ioannis Gerodas (GRE)	147.5 kg./325.00 lbs.

Clean and Jerk
	Total
1. Yuri Zakharevich (URS)	230.0 kg./507.00 lbs.
2. Anton Baraniak (TCH)	225.0 kg./496.00 lbs.
3. Norberto Oberburger (ITA)	215.0 kg./473.75 lbs.
4. Istvan Sandor (HUN)	205.0 kg./451.75 lbs.
5. Jozef Jacso (HUN)	200.0 kg./440.75 lbs.
6. Stanislav Malysa (POL)	197.5 kg./435.25 lbs.
7. Frank Hartmann (GDR)	190.0 kg./418.75 lbs.
8. Ken Clark (USA)	107.5 kg./413.25 lbs.

Super Heavyweight +110 kg./+242.50 lbs.

Overall
	Total
1. Leonid Taranenko (URS)	447.5 kg./986.50 lbs.
2. Aleksandr Gunyashev (URS)	435.0 kg./959.00 lbs.
3. Robert Skolimowski (POL)	397.5 kg./876.25 lbs.
4. Valentin Gyurov (BUL)	387.5 kg./854.25 lbs.
5. John Bergman (USA)	367.5 kg./810.00 lbs.
6. Peter Hudecek (TCH)	355.0 kg./782.50 lbs.
7. Richard Eaton (USA)	345.0 kg./760.50 lbs.

Snatch
	Total
1. Leonid Taranenko (URS)	202.5 kg./446.25 lbs.
2. Aleksandr Gunyashev (URS)	200.0 kg./440.75 lbs.
3. Robert Skolimowski (POL)	177.5 kg./391.25 lbs.
4. Valentin Gyurov (BUL)	175.0 kg./385.75 lbs.
5. John Bergman (USA)	172.0 kg./380.25 lbs.
6. Peter Hudecek (TCH)	160.0 kg./352.50 lbs.
7. Richard Eaton (USA)	155.0 kg./341.50 lbs.

Clean and Jerk
	Total
1. Leonid Taranenko (URS)	245.0 kg./540.00 lbs.
2. Aleksandr Gunyashev (URS)	235.0 kg./518.00 lbs.
3. Robert Skolimowski (POL)	220.0 kg./485.00 lbs.
4. Valentin Gyurov (BUL)	212.5 kg./468.25 lbs.
5. Peter Hudecek (TCH)	195.0 kg./429.75 lbs.
6. John Bergman (USA)	195.0 kg./429.75 lbs.
7. Richard Eaton (USA)	190.0 kg./418.75 lbs.

WRESTLING (Freestyle)

Team Competition
1. URS (3-0)	4. MGL (1-2)
2. BUL (2-1)	5. TUR (1-2)
3. USA (2-1)	6. JPN (0-3)

Individual Competition

Paperweight 48kg./106 lbs.
1. Vasili Gogolev (URS)
2. Marian Avramov (BUL)
3. Tumendemberei Sukhbaatar (MGL)

Flyweight 52kg./115 lbs.
1. Vladimir Toguzov (URS)
2. Ivan Tsonov (BUL)
3. Arsiangijn Tsedensodnom (MGL)

Bantamweight 57kg./126 lbs.
1. Sergei Beloglazov (URS)
2. Kevin Darkus (USA)
3. Stefan Ivanov (BUL)

Featherweight 62kg./137 lbs.
1. John Smith (USA)
2. Khazer Isaev (URS)
3. Alben Kumbarov (BUL)

Lightweight 68kg./150 lbs.
1. Arsen Fadzaev (URS)
2. Andre Metzger (USA)
3. Anguel Sirakov (BUL)

Welterweight 74kg./163 lbs.
1. David Schultz (USA)
2. Adlan Varaev (URS)
3. Rahkmat Sofiyadi (BUL)

Middleweight 82kg./181 lbs.
1. Vladimir Modosyan (URS)
2. Dimitar Markov (BUL)
3. Nedjmi Genchalp (TUR)

Light Weight 90kg./198 lbs.
1. Makharbek Khadartsev (URS)
2. Jim Scherr (USA)
3. Stoyan Nanchev (BUL)

Heavyweight 100kg./220 lbs.
1. Aslan Khadartsev (URS)
2. Hayri Sezgin (TUR)
3. Petio Makedonov (BUL)

Super Heavyweight +100kg./ +220 lbs.
1. Bruce Baumgartner (USA)
2. David Gobedzhishvili (URS)
3. Atanas Atanassov (BUL)

YACHTING

Women's Boardsailing Class
	Points
1. Kathy Steele (USA)	11.7
Joanna Buzinska (POL)	11.7
3. Yulia Kazakova (URS)	14.0
4. Gabriela Kredbova (TCH)	42.0
5. Karolina Boyadzhieva (BUL)	49.4
6. Monique Fechino (ARG)	51.7
7. Cynthia Knot (BRA)	55.0
8. Sharmain McDermid (BOT)	67.7

Women's 470 Class
	Points
1. Karen Johnson (CAN)	6.0
2. Pease Herndon (USA)	17.1
3. Larisa Moskalenko (URS)	20.4
4. Peggy Harwiger (GDR)	32.7
5. Ester Harangyi (HUN)	40.0
6. Wieslawa Hszowanska (POL)	56.4
7. Maria Amelia Dominguez (POR)	57.4

Men's Boardsailing Class
	Points
1. Yevgeni Bogatyryov (URS)	14.7
2. Michael Gebhart (USA)	19.7
3. Marcel Reitsema (HOL)	28.1
4. Richard Muerscaugh (CAN)	31.0
5. Uwe Schmidt (FRG)	37.4
6. Gregori Myszkowski (POL)	56.4
7. Vesa Lehtinen (FIN)	61.1
8. Rose Campbell (AUS)	66.7

Men's 470 Class
	Points
1. Morgan Reeser (USA)	3.7
2. Bernd Hoelt (GDR)	25.4
3. Nigel Cochrane (CAN)	30.0
4. Tynu Tyniste (URS)	32.4
5. Craig Eerris (AUS)	42.1
6. Jean-Charles Scale (FRA)	46.4
7. Andrzej Michalczyk (POL)	48.7
8. Victor Tavers-Schneider (BRA)	56.0

Star Class
	Points
1. Mark Reynolds (USA)	3.0
2. Guram Biganishvili (URS)	9.0

Tornado Class
	Points
1. Yuri Konovalov (URS)	6.0
2. Skip Elliott (USA)	20.4
3. Lars Grael (BRA)	28.1
4. Rex Sellers (NZL)	30.4

Finn
	Points
1. Oleg Khopyorsky (URS)	0.0
2. Dirk Pittelkov (GDR)	17.4
3. Buzz Reynolds (USA)	27.4
4. Antal Szekevbi (HUN)	39.7
5. Jaroslav Marciuk (POL)	41.0
6. Michael Maier (TCH)	46.1
7. Vesa Lehtinen (FIN)	61.1
8. Jorge Garcia-Velasco (ARG)	69.0

Flying Dutchman Class
	Points
1. Aleksandr Shpilko (URS)	0.0
2. J.R. Braun (USA)	22.4
3. Frank McLaughlin (CAN)	32.4
4. Bodo Borowski (GDR)	33.4
5. Kaarlo Brummer (FIN)	40.7
6. Botond Littke (HUN)	43.7

Soling Class
	Points
1. Gyorgi Shaiduko (URS)	11.7
John Kostecki (USA)	11.7
3. Gyorgi Finasi (HUN)	20.4
4. Dimitrios Delegianis (GRE)	51.7

US water polo team captain and Goodwill Ambassador, Terry Schroeder.

PHOTOGRAPHIC CREDITS

AMERICAN

William Hart — 1; 4; 5; 8; 9; 10; 13; 15; 18; 22-U, LL; 24, 25-L; 27-UR; 32; 36; 37; 38; 39; 44; 51; 52-L; 56; 57; 58-LL; 61-UR; 62; 63; 64; 65-L; 68; 70; 71-U; 72-L; 73; 74; 82; 83; 84; 85; 86; 88; 89; 90; 91; 92; 93; 99; 100; 101; 102; 104; 107-R; 108; 109; 113; 114; 116; 118-L; 119; 120; 128; 144; 148; 149; 150; 151; 152; 153; 154; 156-L; 157-U; 159; 160-U; 185; 192.

Dan Helms — 6; 11; 20-U, LL; 23-UR; 25-U; 26; 27; 28; 29; 31; 33; 34; 35; 34 UL; 35 UR; 42; 45; 46; 47; 47 UR; 48; 49; 50; 53; 54; 55; 58-U, LR; 59; 60-U; 61-UL, L; 65-UL, UR; 66; 67; 72-U; 75-L; 94; 95; 96; 97; 98; 103; 110-L; 112; 115; 117; 118-U; 121; 122; 123; 124; 125; 126; 129; 130; 131; 132; 133; 134; 135; 136; 137; 142; 143; 145; 146; 147; 161-U; 170; 171; 172; 173; 181-U; 189.

Phil Huber — 76; 77; 78; 79; 80; 81.

Adam Loory — 16; 162; 164; 165-L; 167; 168-L.

Kelly Mills — 17; 19; 21-LL; 23-L; 30; 52-R; 60-L; 75-U; 158; 160-L; 161-L; 174; 175; 176; 178-L, R; 179; 180-UR, L; 181.

Barbara Y. E. Pyle — 168-U.

Corky Trewin — 12; 43; 71-L; 87-U; 110-U, L; 111-U, L; 127; 183.

SOVIET

Robert I Mairnov — 7; 138; 139; 140; 141.

David Makchmob — 163; 166; 169.

Yuri Sokolov — 186.

Additional photographs were contributed by: **John Bevilaqua** — 20-LC; 177. C and R. **Marge McDonald** — 46-U; 165-U; 177-L; 180-UL.

OPENING PHOTOGRAPHS

Page 2 & 3 – Pressing on in the 10,000 meters are Domingos Castro (347), and Fernando Conto (345) of Portugal, Mark Nenow (443) of the USA, Dionisio Castro (348) of Portugal, and Shunicht Yoneschige (64) of Japan.

Page 4 – America's Cheryl Miller adorns her gold medal with "stars and stripes."

Page 5 – Soviet Sergei Bubka launches himself toward the stars for another world record.

Page 6 – American judoka Steve Cohen enroute the finals and a silver medal.

Page 7 – Women's singles gold medalist Caroline Kuhlman of the U.S.

Page 8 – Debi Thomas treats the audience to her world championship form.

Page 9 – An American backstroker leaves a cascading arch in her wake.

Page 10 – A blurring pace was set in the men's sprints.

Page 11 – The regal Edwin Moses clears another hurdle of track and field history.

Page 12 – A fencer at rest.

Page 13 – The poise, power and beauty of Sweden's Monica Westen.

Page 25 – In an Opening Ceremony's tribute to the 1975 in-space rendezvous of the USA's Apollo and the USSR's Soyuz space crafts, Apollo Commander Thomas Stafford (far left) is reunited with the Soyuz' cosmonauts.